Ian Stark.

To be a
Farmer's Boy

For Irene

To be a
Farmer's Boy
—— G.K. NELSON ——

ALAN SUTTON

First published in 1991 by Alan Sutton Publishing Ltd

First published in this edition in the United Kingdom in 1992 by
Alan Sutton Publishing Ltd · Phoenix Mill · Far Thrupp
Stroud · Gloucestershire

First published in this edition in the United States of America
in 1992 by Alan Sutton Publishing Inc. · Wolfeboro Falls
NH 03896–0848

British Library Cataloguing in Publication Data

Nelson, Geoffrey K. (Geoffrey Kenneth) *1923–*
To be a farmer's boy.
1. Great Britain, Rural regions. Social life, history.
1901–1945
I. Title
942.009734

ISBN 0-7509-0182-9

Library of Congress Cataloging in Publication Data
applied for

*Cover illustration: Boy with team of oxen, Southrop,
photograph by Percy Simms. (Cotswold Countryside
Collection at Northleach (Cotswold District Council))*

Typeset in 11/13 Bembo.
Typesetting and origination by
Alan Sutton Publishing Limited.
Printed in Great Britain by
The Bath Press, Avon.

CONTENTS

ACKNOWLEDGEMENTS

I am grateful to all the four hundred people who wrote in response to my appeal for information, and in particular to those who gave permission to publish either the written material, a transcript of their taped material or the photographs they sent.

I am grateful for the financial assistance given by Birmingham Polytechnic, where I was employed during the initial stages of this project. I am also grateful for the help given by Mrs Mary Sparks in that stage of the work; for the assistance of my daughter-in-law, Mrs Christina Nelson, in typing the material and my wife for proof-reading.

The Farmer's Boy

The sun had set behind yon hill,
across a dreary moor.
When weary and lame a boy there came
up to the farmer's door.
'Can you tell me where ever there be,
one that will me employ.
To plough and sow and reap and mow,
and be a farmer's boy.

'My father's dead, my mother's left
with five children large and small,
and what is worse for my mother still,
I'm the biggest of them all.
Tho' little I am I would labour hard
If I could get employ
To plough and sow and reap and mow
and be a farmer's boy.

'And if that you no boy do want.
one favour I've to ask.
If you'll shelter me till break of day.
From this cold winter's blast.
At the break of day I will haste away
Elsewhere to seek employ
To plough and sow and reap and mow
and be a farmer's boy.'

TO BE A FARMER'S BOY

The farmer's wife cried 'Try the lad
Let him no longer seek,'
'Yes, father, do,' the daughter cried.
While the tears rolled down her cheek.
'For those who would work it's hard to want,
and wander for employ.
Don't let him go, but let him stay
and be a farmer's boy.'

The farmer's boy grew up a man
and the good old couple died.
They left the lad the farm they had
and their daughter for his bride.
Now the lad that was, and the farm now has,
often thinks and smiles with joy
and blesses the day he came that way
To be a farmer's boy.

Traditional

PREFACE

As one grows older there is a tendency to look back on the past; having arrived at that stage of life I thought that it was time I began to attempt to record the life-style of the past, a style that has now disappeared. Of course I could have depended entirely on my own memories and written an autobiography, but I felt that I needed to confirm my own memories by comparing them with those of my contemporaries. I was particularly interested in country life as I was born and brought up in a tied cottage on a farm in Norfolk in the 1920s.

I was unable to travel long distances, and since I wanted to get information that would enable me to compare the way of life in different parts of the country in the first half of the present century I decided to write to a number of country newspapers appealing to their readers for information. I was surprised by the response, for I received over four hundred replies all of which contained some valuable information. Of course these communications varied widely in both length and depth. Some amounted to short autobiographies, indeed a few were not that short, and one was over ten thousand words in length. Some were short accounts of particular incidents or provided detailed information on a specific aspect of farming or village life. These all arrived either as handwritten records or taped accounts.

Most of my informants were either small farmers, farm workers or their wives and daughters and it was interesting to note the considerable literary quality, the high standard of spelling and the legibility of the handwriting of people who had left school at the age of fourteen or even earlier. Many of the accounts received were of such intrinsic interest that they warranted publication both as historical records and as personal stories.

Unlike most information obtained through the methods of oral historical research, I did not ask specific questions of my informants, simply requesting that they would send me their reminiscences. The reason for this was that I was interested in obtaining spontaneous accounts, as far as possible uninfluenced by the biases of the researcher. What do people remember of the past, as they sit and think back over their own lives? And what conclusion can be reached from the stories they tell?

I decided to select a representative sample of the longer and most coherent stories to present a comprehensive picture of farming and country life during the first half of the century from the point of view of farm workers, and which was told, as far as possible, in their own words.

A major problem arose from the necessity to choose a small sample from the available material. For this volume I decided to restrict my sample to male English farm workers, with the intention of producing later volumes on women, children and farmers. I also decided that contributions should be selected in such a way that they represented different regions of the country and reflected the various types of farming practised in the areas chosen.

I have tried to minimize the amount of editing in order to allow my informants to speak for themselves, but some editing has been necessary to prevent duplication of material between informants, and repetition within each individual story.

The book is illustrated with photographs sent by correspondents and material collected by the editor.

Following a general introduction which sets the scene within which the actors play their parts, the story of each of the informants is presented in his own words.

INTRODUCTION

The first half of the twentieth century saw many changes in the economic fortune of Britain and in the social life of its people. Economic and technological change was rapid and affected all levels of society, including those who worked on the land. One of the most conspicuous changes in the style of life of the countrymen has been the reduction of the isolation that so marked the condition of life at the beginning of the century. Of course, even then rural communities were not so isolated as they had been a century earlier, before the introduction of the railway, but even at the height of the golden age of the railways many villages were remote from the nearest railway station. Roads were poor and the motor car was only just beginning to appear. In the years up to the Second World War few people in the average village possessed a car – the squire, the doctor, a wealthy farmer and perhaps the parson. The smaller farmers still depended on horse-drawn transport as did the local tradesmen. The farm workers either walked or used a bicycle.

The average farm worker seldom went far from his village except to go to the nearest small market town on market day once a week. Naturally some workers moved from one village to another to find a job, but this was not easy because most houses were 'tied cottages' owned by farmers who reserved them for their own employees. This had one advantage in that if you were offered a job you were guaranteed a house, but it also meant that if you lost your job you usually also lost your house since the farmer would need it for the man who was replacing you. My maternal grandfather moved six or seven times during his working life, usually to improve his position, but my paternal grand-parents spent all their lives in the same village in which their ancestors had lived for over a century, and they were more typical of the general run of country workers.

The opportunities for travel were limited not only because of the inadequacy of transport but also by the fact that farm workers had no holidays apart from Christmas Day and some bank holidays. Up to the Second World War we went to the seaside at Wells-Next-The-Sea perhaps twice a year for a day trip when we visited my great aunt who lived there. We also had an annual day trip to Great Yarmouth usually with a charabanc party, and we even went to Norwich on rare visits by train. In 1939 my father had the first paid week's holiday of his life and we had just returned home when war broke out.

Not only were farm workers limited in the extent to which they travelled, but their knowledge of the outside world was limited by the low standard of education. This was particularly the case with my grandparents' generation. My maternal grandfather (Walter Pitcher) remained illiterate all his life, having had only one year of 'schooling', at the time when children were charged 1d. a week to go to school. He was the eldest of a family of thirteen, his parents could not afford to keep him at school so he was sent to work on the farm at the age of seven. By the age of eleven he was in charge of a team of horses and he eventually rose to become a farm steward (manager), in charge of a large farm of over one thousand acres. My grandmother who had received a better education could write and kept the farm accounts for him.

My father's generation received a free elementary education, but he left school at the age of thirteen and went to work on the farm. Later he obtained a job in the malt-house in the village of Great Ryburgh where he lived. Conditions were very bad when he was a boy during the Great Depression at the end of the nineteenth century, and the family often went hungry. He was sent out at night to get turnips from the fields, for, since his father also worked at the malt-house they did not get any of the perks given to farm workers. The old men of the village would pay a boy to read the newspaper to them in the pub at night when my father was a boy. So news of the outer world was beginning to influence the minds and lives of country folk as the new century dawned.

When the twentieth century began British agriculture had been going through a period of decline for some twenty-five years, a period known to historians as the Great Depression. The main reason for the decline of agriculture at that time was the increase in the quantity of food being imported from abroad. Brown (1987) estimated that there was a fall of 13.5 per cent in agricultural production in England between 1870 and 1900. While there seems to have been some slight recovery in the early years of the century only 42 per cent of the food consumed in the United Kingdom in 1914 was produced here.

During the Depression the number of workers on the land decreased and workers left the villages in search of work in the towns. As an example we may take my maternal great-grandfather, William Pitcher, who left his native village for London where he found a job as a horseman in Hyde Park. All his family went with him with the exception of my grandfather, Walter, who had married when he was nineteen and was settled in a job, and one daughter who had also married.

During the early years of the century agricultural wages averaged about thirteen shillings a week. How did a family manage to live on such a small income? L. Marion Springall (1936) gives an example of a Norfolk labourer's budget for 1913, for a family of five.

'Of the 14 shillings wage 3d. goes to insurance. The man keeps 9d. for 'beer and baccy'. The wife's expenditure is as follows:

2 stone flour	3s. 6d.
1 lb. butter	3s. 6d.
1 lb. cheese	10d.
3 lb. port	2s. 3d.
¼ lb. tea	6d.
Matches	1d.
Soap	3d.
Starch	1d.

Candles .... 2d.
Oil .... 4d.
Sundries .... 8d.
1 cwt Coal .... 1s. 3d.
Sugar .... 4d.
....
                                                    11s. 6d.

This leaves 6d. for the club for boots and clothing.'

It was a tight budget that left no room for luxuries or savings, but this was the way our ancestors lived. No allowance was made for rent so we must assume that this worker was living rent free in a tied cottage. Not all tied cottages were rent free, the farmer usually making a small charge which might be deducted from the wage paid. Many workers would get other small perks such as free milk and potatoes, and most of them would grow all the vegetables they used in their own gardens, keep chickens, both for eggs and meat, and a pig.

The First World War led to an increase in prosperity for farmers. Agriculture flourished, wages rose and the number of workers employed on the land increased. The need for additional labour, not only to offset the numbers of men recruited into the forces but also to boost production was to a large extent met by the recruitment of women workers. While many of these were countrywomen including farm workers' wives, a large number were townswomen with no knowledge of farming who joined the Women's Land Army. Another source of labour was found in the prisoners of war.

The reason for the growth of agriculture in wartime was related to the difficulties of importing foodstuffs from abroad. One difficulty was the lack of money to pay for imports since British manufacturers had to change from the production of goods for export to the production of war materials. The second factor was the shortage of shipping caused by the German submarine campaign on the one hand and the need to use available ships for the import of goods essential to the war effort. The government subsidized food production thus improving the farmers' incomes. However, this all ceased when the war ended and in the twenties and thirties farming again suffered depression as the importation of foreign foods once more made home production uneconomic.

The decline of prosperity of the farmers was, of course, passed on to the workers. One way of cutting the costs of production is to cut wages and the average rate of pay fell from 42s. a week in 1920 to 25s. a week in 1923 for a fifty-hour week. This reduced the real standard of living to about what it had been in 1913. At the same time farmers were demanding a longer working week. In Norfolk, where the National Union of Agricultural workers was strong and effectively organized, a strike was called. While neither side got what they wanted the union was successful in preventing any further reduction in wages or increases in working hours. The success of the Norfolk strike led to a stabilization of conditions throughout the country.

In 1924 the Labour government established the Central Wages Board and County Wages Committees that had the job of fixing the wage rate in each of the counties. As a result wage rates varied from one country to another but on the whole wage rates increased everywhere. To take again the case of Norfolk, wage rates increased from 25s. to 29s. for a summertime week of fifty hours and to 28s. for a winter week of forty-eight hours. By 1938 this had risen to 34s. and 6d. Higher rates were paid for the more skilled workers. In Norfolk, cowmen were paid 6s. 6d. more and team men and shepherds 5s. 6d. more (see 'Further reading', R. Groves).

During the 1930s many farm workers lost their jobs for a number of reasons. In the first place, some farmers went bankrupt and because their land could not be sold for farming the farms became derelict. Other farmers were able to survive by changing their style of farming, for example, from cereal production to milk production, or in suitable areas to horticulture and market gardening. The new type of farming affected the number and type of workers required. Finally, the introduction of new machinery was a major cause of the reduction of labour, though this became a more significant factor during and after the Second World War.

The fall in the number of workers was reflected in the membership of the National Union of Agricultural Workers which fell from a peak of 126,000 in 1919 to 30,000 in the early 1930s. The desperate situation faced by agriculture in the early thirties induced the government to take some action and in 1932 a system of subsidies was introduced followed by the establishment of marketing boards, including the Milk Marketing Board which started work in 1933.

Agriculture began to recover from the Depression in the late thirties, though full recovery did not occur until the outbreak of the Second World War when the situation again gave rise to a need to maximize the production of food. The demand for an improvement in efficiency led to a rapid increase in mechanization which has continued since the war and has produced a condition which may well be called factory farming. The effect of commercialization and mechanization is the subject of much comment by the contributors to this book as they look back to an age when most farms were worked by the farmer together with his family and a few hired workers.

With regard to the social conditions, life in the villages has undergone considerable change. Rural areas have become urbanized and in many respects the life of the countryman has become almost indistinguishable from that of the townsfolk. This has been the result of the introduction of amenities such as electricity and a piped water supply. The introduction of electricity has had the greatest impact, for not only has it replaced oil lamps and candles as a means of lighting, but it has also replaced coal as a means of heating and of powering machinery. It has also made labour-saving devices such as cleaners and washing machines as readily available to the country dweller as to those who live in towns and, most important of all, it has made possible the rapid communication of information and news from the outside world. The telephone has made personal communication over longer distances so much easier, while the radio, and later the television, have brought news and information about the outer world into the homes of country folk to an extent unthought of at the beginning of the century.

INTRODUCTION

The railway system reached the height of its expansion in the inter-war period but it was already being supplemented by the development of regular bus services which carried on the process of urbanization not only by making the towns more accessible to the rural population, but also by opening up the countryside to the town dweller and increasingly serving to convert villages into dormitories for urban workers. However, the effect of these developments was limited until the post Second World War period when they were hastened by the increased availability of the private motor car.

The cumulative effect of all these developments has been to change the character of rural life so that it will seem to younger generations, living in the nineties, as alien as that of the ancient Romans or of tribal societies in Africa before the coming of the white man.

Indeed my grandfather had more in common with a British peasant at the time of the Roman occupation than with a farm worker of the present day. The inter-war period was the last period in which it was possible to experience a truly rural style of life in England, a period in which machines were still marginal and most work was carried out by hand or with the assistance of horses.

CHAPTER ONE

CHANGE ON THE SUSSEX DOWNS

Our understanding of the present is conditioned by our experience of the past, but as we grow older we tend to judge the present in terms of the past and perhaps to see the past through 'rose-coloured spectacles'. Have the changes that have occurred during the past fifty years been for the better or for the worse? In some respects most people are far better off in material terms, but we are beginning to realize that we have also lost much of value in the process.
Mr L.F.M. Clarke of Lancing sent me an excellent account of the changes that have taken place on the Sussex Downs from which I quote at length.

Up to 1950 the farming areas of the Downs and coastal plains of Sussex were basically mixed farms, though some were specialized, with grade 'A' milking herds and others with beef cattle. Because the north scarp of the Downs is so steep it was impossible to use it for anything other than keeping sheep.

Rabbits abounded and a walk on the Downs could be compared with a walk on a large well kept lawn. Up to thirty species of plants grew to the square foot and each footstep would put the scent of a number of these into the air. It was a pleasant experience to walk, or to work with these conditions underfoot. Most farms consisted of a series of small fields bounded by hedges or streams in the river valleys. The hillsides were littered with small coppices, often with rides cut into them for shooting parties.

The fields would be crop-rotated to produce hay. Clover would be sown, the first crop often thrashed for seed, the second crop dried and harvested for fodder, sheep would be grazed on the third crop which would then be ploughed in to prepare for winter wheat.

Pigs were kept in sties where there was a supply of swill, but sometimes they were put out in a field or an orchard in winter. Most farms had a flock of sheep, the shepherd usually having a cottage on the hillside. Mustard grown for seed was then fenced off with hurdles and used as sheep fodder. The horse was the only motive power on the farm up to the late 1930s. Fields were ploughed, harrowed, rolled and sown by horse-drawn implements, and at harvest time the self-binder would also be horse-drawn.

Threshing was done by a steam-powered drum. The fields were weeded for docks and thistles by hand. Fields seem to have been based on a size so that it was a day's work to harvest them.

The first real machinery seen on a lot of farms was the giro-tiller, diesel-powered and not unlike a traction engine with two large disks at the back and spade legs attached. These were lowered into the earth and rotated as the machine drove across the field. This job was usually done by a contractor, no local farmers owned one personally. Some fields, especially on low ground had been ploughed at one time by a cable-drawn plough with a machine on each side of the field.

Each farm had a staff of cowmen, carters, shepherds and often a stockman for pigs, and general labourers who did ditching, hedging and general maintenance, beside helping with the general running of the farm.

Most of the staff lived on the farm in cottages which were basic dwellings. Few had power or gas, water or drains. But the farm worker of pre-war days was able to run the farm without help from outside, apart from the thresher who was usually a contractor because of the cost of the machinery involved for the short amount of time it was used – perhaps only a week per farm.

One of the doubtful pleasures of a youngster's life at that time was to visit the local shepherd who did not normally live within the farm confines. The door would open and a ruddy-faced bearded giant would say, 'Come on in'. 'Mother give the lad a glass of wine.' Two glasses of what appeared to be a colourless liquid would be served on a tray by an apron-clad mature woman who could wring washing drier with her bare hands than the average spin-drier of today. The shepherd would drink this liquid with the ease of a Wimbledon tennis player consuming a glass of lemon barley, but woe betide the youth that attempted the same feat. He would be of the opinion that burning petrol was being poured down his throat, while his ears had left his head with a loud roar, and his legs would suddenly tremble like those of a puppet on a string. As the lad's eyes began to see through the mist and tears he would be aware of another glass being offered, 'That's it lad, drink up'. It was a good fortune of architecture that the way home was usually down hill. The old farm wife seemed to be able to make wine out of almost anything.

The wartime advance of machinery meant that the single ploughshare of the horse was superseded by the three to five ploughshares of the tractor-drawn machine. This meant that a large proportion of the grubs were buried and not eaten by the gulls, and consequently tractor-drawn insecticide sprayers were developed.

Carters were not always of the age where they could become tractor drivers and so they became redundant. The north scarp of the Downs could now be ploughed, and large machines pulled up and burned the coppices. Sheep were no longer kept and the shepherd dis-appeared. I do not want to talk about subsidies and corn mountains, but it was not long before hedges dis-appeared, the cattle went and the cowmen became redundant.

Now at harvest time the combines are hired from a contractor. There is no need for stooking or shocking up as it is called and the general farm labourer has sought other employment. The hedgerows that lined the streams were a source of blackberries, hips and sloes. They were no problem when the stream was cleaned out by a farm-hand with a long-handled ditching tool. But the mechanical digger soon cleared all in its path and made an extra three foot per field for corn crops. By now farm cottages were being bought by the wealthy as weekend retreats and were modernized. The farm-hand had raised a large family in these cottages, but in order to be able to sit and watch television in the evenings or have a few friends in at weekends someone was prepared to spend many times the original cost of these dwellings to have a light switch and a water tap with all the available accessories.

The combine harvesters grew in size and the fields became larger by removing hedges, trees and fences. A farm which had twenty fields in the thirties had only four or five in the seventies. The farm staff dwindled to the tractor driver, who repaired what fencing was left or maintained the granaries during his non-driving spells. Even now some local farms are entirely contractor managed and ploughing, sowing, spraying and combining are all done by contracted companies. I am not too sure that many of the old carters had a pilot's licence to do the aerial spraying seen on the Downs now!

As I said before, a walk on the Downs forty years ago was a pleasant experience, like walking over a lawn. Now one treads a rut-filled track bordered by five strands of barbed wire. There are no hares or pheasants; rabbits and partridges are rare and the whole of the hillside and every valley is corn – a vast desert of brownish yellow in the autumn sun. As the combines complete their task, straw which was once put in a rick and used as bedding in stalls and stables or spread in a bullock yard to be later piled in great heaps to rot as the basis for a successful crop the following season, is now burnt. The whole of the Sussex sky is one dark cloud and the morning finds burnt particles of straw in all the streets. For several winters now several villages like Rottingdean have been inundated with mud after the heavy rains. In some places there is less than a foot of soil on top of solid chalk and there is nothing to bind the soil together. People who have never been on a farm in their lives are suddenly the victims of modern farming methods: their garden walls and cars covered while the local firemen try to stem the flood with an endless filling of sandbags.

I think the odd farm hand required to run a modern farm lives in the nearest town and goes to work by car. The old country cottage's vegetable garden is now a garage and the reproduction ancient lamp housing an electric light bulb over the porch has replaced the glow of the paraffin lamp in the kitchen. The village pub now sells more fillet steaks than it sold pints of beer in the thirties.

Cud-chewing cattle, nervous flocks of sheep and furious looking bulls are now merely ghosts among vast areas of corn, and not a hedge in sight. The Sussex farm hand could now be a garage mechanic; he certainly will never be asked to thatch a rick or build a potato clamp.

CHAPTER TWO

A LANCASHIRE LIFE

From the Downs of Sussex we go north to Lancashire to hear the story of the life of Mr Charles Simpson (1892–1984). I never had the pleasure of meeting him, but his grandson Mr John Simpson sent me the following transcripts of tape recordings made by Charles; they give a brief but vivid account of his life between 1892 and the 1930s.

I was born at a hill farm above Grindleton, called Whitestones on 4 July 1892. We moved from there when I were one year old to a farm called Old Greenwoods a little bit lower down. My father he were a farmer. There was a big family of us, eighteen children. There were thirteen of us brought up. I'd three brothers and three sisters older and three brothers and three sisters younger than me. My dad went out to work besides farming. There wasn't a lot of money in farming in them days. There wasn't a milk board, it were just butter-making and calf rearing . . . I remember eggs being 10d. a dozen. I remember tobacco being 3d. an ounce. We killed a couple of pigs a year and had ham and bacon for twelve months.

I went to a little school at Lane End in 1896. It had thirty-two scholars. I were four and a half years old when I started school. I went in frock and petticoats. There wasn't a pair of pants available for me. They used to hand 'em down from one to t'other and they wasn't just ready for another pair.

We used to have Lane End's tea party the week before Christmas when school was broke up. I were allus the chief reciter. I could learn any poem quicker than any o't'others. I used to recite at Lane End and at Holden Chapel. Allus on Christmas Day they had their tea party. Four o'clock for t'scholars and again at night for t'concert and then supper after. And what great days they were. Everything home-baked. Those ladies would have a big basket under t'table piled up with all good things. It was a real treat, and they carry that on to this day.

It were all right in summer but in winter when stock were all inside it were a great push for t'farmers from these outlying farms. Two or three miles each way they'd come. Service started at half past one and finished about three. They'd come out and rush home and get back into their working clothes and then be back for seven o'clock at night, and they thought nothing about walking in them days. Now if they have a hundred yards to go they've to have a motor car to go it in. When we were in farm service they used to pack us a lunch up and we took it with us and ate it. They had facilities for brewing tea and we used to have our dinner in t'Sunday school between morning Sunday school and afternoon.

On Collop Monday these farm lads used to meet at Lane Ends, black their faces with soot out t'chimney, turn their jackets wrong side out and go round t'farms;

'Please a collop.' And those farmers' wives would give 'em some bacon. Four or five farms they went round and finished up at one farm and that farmer's wife used to cook 'em this bacon and put 'em an egg or two in and they had a jolly good feed and that allus happened on t'Monday before Pancake Tuesday. And then there were Mischief Night. I think that were about end of October. They used to go round t'farms – never did any real damage, never broke a thing – they might take a wheelbarrow and put it into a quarry somewhere or take a wheel off a cart and hide that, or things like that. Farmers thought nothing of it. They'd look round, find their tackle and put it together again. It were a bit of energy they wanted to get shot of, that's all.

I left school when I was twelve years of age. I passed a special inspector's test. I was needed at home that year because my mother were on her deathbed and it was lambing time and I had to look after the sheep.

When I was thirteen (in 1905) I went into farm service on a farm across the way called Greaves. I was there two years. My first wage was £10 for a year and I lived in, of course. I worked for Thomas Balshaw. He used to have 'bits o' does' of going off and getting drunk and I was left in charge for two or three days sometimes. Lambing time I'd be going round the fields at eleven o'clock at night with a lantern. Come in and t'Missus said, 'Get to bed now. You'll have to be up t'crows piss.'

I said, 'What time's that?'

She said, 'Four o'clock. That's what time t'crows piss. You'll have to be out and go round t'sheep.'

Then we had to milk cows at three different places giving a drop of milk each and I used to go round with a carrying kit on my back from one to another and get home about breakfast time at nine o'clock. That were my daily round till lambing time finished and t'boss got back to work.

From there I went to my uncle's place at Higher Cross. I were there three years. A very nice place, I allus had a good place in farm service. My dad said, 'Keep t'reight side of t'Missus and you'll not have a bad shop' and it allus happened that way. When I was at Higher Cross with my uncle they decided to build an extra Sunday school to Holden Chapel. My father were mason for t'job, he did all the stonework. When they were digging t'foundations out they'd all this soil to cart away and tip down into t'river. And we found an old mare at Higher Cross, a real old cranky mare. She'd either kick or bite or do anything but I got reight friendly with her. I could do anything with her. I said, 'Well, I'll go and fetch th'old mare and t'cart. Ay, tha mornt bring that thing here.' Anyhow, I went and fetched her down and could do anything. I could back her up just where we wanted. Nobody dare go near her head, and foreman, like, he kept watching this job. He said, 'It's best team we have here.' There were another horse and cart beside mine but I could just back her up where I wanted. She never stirred till I got hold of her head, but by gum, when you used to start yoking her she'd get her hind leg up like she was going to kick, and if you passed that she'd turn round with her mouth going to bite you. She never once touched me. I could walk past her. T'other horse what we had was supposed to be quiet and I were frightened to death of it. This old mare would kick her own foal. We'd to take her shoes off before she foaled so she didn't harm it. She were a real worker. She could mow, and I could back loads of hay into t'barn. Her teeth would be going, she'd be gnashing her teeth but she were all reight.

I finished up with £18 a year at my uncle's but I weren't satisfied so I went to Gisburn at £24 a year. I were there four years and finished up at £31 a year. That were t'top wage in them days for a qualified man (between 1910 and 1914). For the first two years I were t'cowman and for the second two years I were t'horse-man. We used to break in about two horses a year and sell 'em when they got nicely settled down. And you didn't get paid for overtime. You used to walk these horses out a t'spring o' year at nights when you'd finished your work. Walk 'em round on long reins for a start and then you'd get 'em shod and started to ride 'em and of course you got 'em yoked. And between turning t' cows out and haytime we used to cart coal from Nelson to get t'horses ready for haytime. And if you had a horse and cart with you, you could get a pint of ale, a clay pipe and a box of matches for three ha'pence. That were called a carter's pint.

These horses had never seen a tram in their lives and when you got down to Barrowford you come along among t'trams. You'd have one young horse, two year old, tied at back o' t'cart, a three year old in t'shafts. They'd never seen a tram and you didn't know how to do to get past, but do t'best you could. I had one jump on to a garden wall one day but anyhow it didn't do any damage.

It were a grand life in them days. Long hours – we started about a quarter to five in t'morning and finished about half past six at night, and that were regular. In t'summertime we used to get into t'brook or t'river, nearest like, when it were warm weather. That were only time we ever had baths. There were no baths in farmhouses. I can never remember having a bath all the time I were in farm service other than just what we got through t'summertime in t'brook.

When I were at Gisburn we had a lot o' rabbits and there were a shop in Gisburn. We could take 'em and it kept us supplied with tobacco – three of us – for a rabbit. It'd be 10½d. in them days. I remember it going up from 3d. to 3½d. after t'Boer War. Two spinster ladies kept this shop and they didn't use to weigh t'tobacco, they just put it round their necks and broke it off at a certain place – that were an ounce and we got three ounces for a rabbit.

Things have altered a lot in farming since them days. . . . There were no electricity. There were no milking machines. Everything had to be done by hand. There were no muck spreaders, it all had to be carted out in heaps and spread after with t'fork.

It used to be a job groping around doing t'milking with a candle stuck in t'wall or an old lantern. You'd do things the old-fashioned method . . . it were harder work. Farming's easy now to what it were in them days.

We used to wash sheep before clipping time. It were my job one year to get into t'river. You stood up to your armpits in water. It were a jolly cold job. I remember I washed 105 sheep stood in water and then, of course, when I come out they gave me a drop o'whisky and stripped me down and I had a fresh pair o'clothes to put on after.

You'd to be a bit of a vet besides, as well as being a farm worker. There used to be a lot of Irish heifers come over and they used to get felon in the legs and get big, thick joints and we used to what they call rowel 'em. You put a needle through their breast and got some broad tape and put some Venice turpentine on it then put a knot on this tape and drew it through. You cut if off and put another knot on and drew it backwards and forwards with this Venice turpentine on. It set it kind of mattering and every few days you used to pull it backwards and forwards, put some ordinary turpentine and it seemed to clear 'em out. At a certain age these heifers' teeth would start coming loose and a fresh lot coming up and they'd get fangs loose at one side. They got so sore that they couldn't eat. I started feeling in their mouths and I used to pull their tongues out of their mouth as far as I could get it and hold it with one hand so I could get my knife against this offending tooth and my thumb and pull 'em out. I got a fairly good hand at it.

There were nobody worked Sundays in them days. Did as little as they possibly could. There were no such thing as haymaking. You'd work till nearly twelve o'clock at Saturday night and up happen half past two or three o'clock at Monday morning mowing before milking.

When I were t'horseman at Gisburn we bought a young horse for haytime, a three year old, half broken. I met it at Clitheroe and it would neither follow me nor walk in front nor nothing. . . . And a fellow said, 'Get on its back and I'll stick to it.' So I got on its back and rode it home, and weren't I sore. It were a real dud. We couldn't get it into shafts. It wouldn't work in t'traces. It wouldn't pull the chain harrow round the field day after day. Put it in the shafts and it would get one leg over the shafts and stand there. T'Boss said, 'You want to lick it with this stick.' Young Boss gave it a crack at back o'th'ear and it dropped it on t' floor but it did no good, and we'd to turn it out and it never did anything through haytime. So I mowed all t'land – must have been toward seventy acres – with one horse. We'd a two-horse machine but it wouldn't pull at all. We put it between two others but it wouldn't pull an ounce. So th'army were wanting horses in them days but they'd only take 'em a four year old and this were a three year old. So t'Boss said, 'Tell 'em it's a late foal like and it hasn't picked its teeth, Tell 'em it's a four year old'. But it were no good. They just looked into its mouth and said, 'Thank you very much. Take it back home.' So they sent me to Clitheroe Fair with it and said, 'You mun sell it.' So I sold it to some horse-dealer from Barnoldswick for £28.

Of course, there were nothing like balers in them days. I remember going down on to t'meadow one morning about nine o'clock and I were forking loads of hay all day in an eighteen-acre meadow. As soon as I'd finished one cart another cart were waiting for me. That were my job all day. I said to t'boss at night, 'By gum, I'm tired.'

'Why, tha's done nowt,' he says.

We had four Irishmen come helping at haytime when I were at Gisburn. They were all right, as long as they'd plenty o' beer. They used to buy two eighteen-gallons of beer for haytime. They'd be out at four o'clock at t'morning with their scythes and two quart bottles o' ale with them and they were quite happy. 'Sure', they'd say, 'A man cannot live without beer.' They were never no trouble.

We used to get a week's holiday a year. That's what you were allowed. You could have days off occasionally or half days when things weren't so busy. It were a happy life.

Of course, after I got married (1915) we wanted somewhere to live so we started in a little cottage at Rimington and then we moved to Helmshore. And I worked at Tor View Farm, then called Whamshole, for a cattle dealer. I stayed with him about thirteen months. They were long hours then – cows calving, waiting o'cows coming off t'train and one thing and another. It was a hard life so I went to work for another farmer. I were there six years (1916–22). In the meantime I started on a little place called New Barn with about seven or eight acres of land for a start and kept increasing. Then we came to Tor View and since then I've been able to buy the place and I've been semi-retired since I were sixty-five.

CHAPTER THREE

CAMBRIDGESHIRE WAYS

Mr Fred Gambie of Thriplow died in 1987 before I was able to meet him, but his friend Mrs V. Barker of the nearby village of Melbourn sent me a copy of a prize essay he had written on his school days, another essay of his on village life in the 1920s and some further notes he had made. In putting these together into a connected account I have kept to his words only altering in one or two places the sequence, in order to introduce the notes in the appropriate place. The account of his schooldays is of particular interest.

I was born 28 January 1900 and started school in a good church school built in the 1860s on my fifth birthday and left on my thirteenth. The school had a headmistress and two assistant teachers and an average of one hundred pupils. It was kept reasonably warm and there was no modern sanitation, and nowhere to wash your hands. The playground was small and made of flintstones to be trod in by the pupils (there was no tarmac), and if you fell over and grazed your hands or knees one of the older boys would scrape off the mud with his pocket knife. There was no more attention until you got home and one's mother washed it, etc. I've a scar on my leg that's still plain to see which is several inches long, where I fell down in the road and cut it on a flintstone.

I suppose I was an average scholar as there were some better and some not so good. We had a slate to learn to write on and we worked in a smaller room for two or three years, and the ones that done the best work had to march in step to show the headmistress with our slates held high in front of us. We got a smirk from her and a pat on the head or back. When we were older and in her class if we didn't do the work quite so good she used to come behind us as we sat at our desks and dig us in the ribs or crump us on the knuckles with her pointer. Yes they were quite lavish with the punishments. You had to hold out your hand and got two or three stinging strokes with a thin cane. I didn't tell my mother or she would have said you must have deserved it, and many times since I'm glad she let me take it.

The vicar used to come once a week and take a scripture lesson, and one of the first things we had to learn was the Ten Commandments. I wonder what percentage there is do it now. I went in the church choir when I was nine years old, and I can vividly remember going to church with my mother on 23 April 1908 in deep snow for the new organ to be dedicated. There was little or no exams equal to today's eleven plus. I remember one lot of older boys went to the next village, Fowlmere, for exams, but no one went to the county school from here in my time. When we had singing lessons we all had to stand on the long forms and learn them as best we could as we had no copy nor was it written on the blackboard. They were all Scottish songs as our headmistress was Scottish.

Village recreations were few. The fair once a year, bonfire night 5 November and Sunday school treat once a year and if the teachers were not looking we'd start on the cake and make our tea of it. There were swings put up, races to run and scrambles for sweets in the long grass, the vicar used to throw them around [it was not very hygenic and would be frowned upon today]. The roads were covered in mud all winter and it had to be scraped off with long deep hoes, and when it dried in the spring we used to get out our marbles, spinning tops and the wooden and iron hoops and chase them for miles. We sometimes played hopscotch with the girls.

Boys were wanted to help with the horses in harvest time, and if we were too far from home we had our dinners in the field. The boys fed and watered the horses, the men rested, some went to sleep. One man, Mr Flack by name, with his collar loose, felt something down his back. It was a mouse and in his own dialect he said, 'His little ole feet were cold.' I went to work in the summer holidays at nine years old leading horses in the harvest field.

There were very few bicycles about and punctures were frequent with the state of the roads. The first car came in the village about 1912, a Ford where one had to sit bolt upright. The district nurse came around 1910 and anyone wanting her services had to pay a few shillings a year. The council started sending a doctor around the schools about 1912.

In the spring when the corn was sown, we used to go and keep the crows off the corn until it was growing and, in gangs on a Saturday, to hoe the big weeds up for 6d. a day. When I left school they gave me a gun to fire at the crows and I had to stay there till six o'clock.

When you left school there were very few apprenticeships to a trade in those days, and one had to work on the land for 3s. 6d. a week until one could find a better job. It used to be very interesting to go and watch the village blacksmith make the horseshoes and nail them on. For a long time it puzzled me why it didn't hurt. The smithy is still in good condition, a museum now with the forge, new and old shoes and old hand-made tools. I was one of a family of ten born here and all lived to adult age and father got 13s. a week before the First World War. An interesting old custom I must not miss out, singing on Valentine's Day for coppers and sweets at the big houses. We sang,

> Good morning Valentine,
> Curl your locks as I do mine,
> Two before and three behind,
> Say Good morning Valentine.

This was sung several times.

Family life wasn't easy for anyone as large families were the rule rather than the exception. The parents' clothes had to last for years and the children's clothes had to be handed down to the younger ones until they just wouldn't hold together. Beer was 2d. a pint and one could buy a small barrel at 1½d. a pint, that was just at harvest time. Tobacco was 3d. an ounce, cheap cigarettes five for 1d. and, if one was feeling a bit seedy, a nip of whisky for 2d.

As the girls left school at thirteen they had to go into domestic service and one of the brothers went in the army. One went up the north to work as there were two bedrooms for the twelve, including our parents. At one time, about 1905, seven of our family had to be taken to the isolation hospital at Royston with scarlet fever for six weeks. One amusing little incident, as all the village children were going to children's service one Sunday, a tramp was at the bottom of the lane with his stick and his tea can. He said to the vicar could he come to church. The vicar said, 'Yes and you can pick the hymn', that was no. 242, 'We Love The Place O God' [sic]. We didn't take much notice of the parson that day. Another time a boy and I were playing and the chimney sweep stopped and we had to get up on his cart with him and pick walnuts for him for the rest of the day. He said, 'Come down for your money tonight.' We went with great expectations and got 3d.

The milk we had to fetch from the village dairy before breakfast. Skimmed milk was ½d. and full cream was 1d. We learned to smoke when we were eleven years old. When we came out of Sunday school we used to take it in turns to pay ½d. each to buy Woodbines five for 1d. and go down the Brook Road for a smoke. The only toy I ever had was a 6d. clockwork motor my eldest sister bought me. The only Easter egg I ever had was a chocolate one the vicar's daughter bought me and she took my photo standing in the road. I was seven years old and I've still got it. When anyone wanted the right time we used to check the clock in the Post Office as the postmaster used to have the time come through by telephone at nine o'clock in the morning. Anyone working in the field and hadn't got a watch used to listen for hooters, one at Shepreth and one at Whittlesford morning, midday, and when it was time to stop work at night.

There was a pair of cottages built – date in them 1875 – and I've checked all the other houses in the village and there couldn't have been any more built until 1921 when the first four council houses were built.

Before the days of the farm tractor there were eighty-five to one hundred horses in the village including the young ones in training. In the summer when the horses were out in the meadows, if there was a heavy thunderstorm in the night the horse-keepers used to call them and put them in the stables to get them away from the trees.

We would get a trip to Cambridge once a year when the harvest sales were on. We got there by the carrier's cart or walk to Harston station three miles away. On August bank holiday on Midsummer Common there was a large fair known as the Mammoth Show and on the outskirts of the village we could see the parachute coming down from the balloon; that was as near as I got to it.

The Church

Lots of people used to go to church and the lads used to be proud to be in the choir. I always remember my first choir supper at nine years old. The wine was poured out to drink a toast, no one told me not to drink yet and I tipped it up. When the others drank the toast I had to lift up an empty glass and pretend. Not many people go to church now but they must still be good at heart because when there is a fête or anything to raise money for the church there's always willing helpers. When there was a Confirmation service in a nearby village they used to get there in a farm wagon drawn by two horses. We went to Shepreth station the same way when we had a day at Lowestoft, the only day I had at the seaside as a child, which was a Band of Hope outing. There was a Band of Hope meeting once a week in the winter when we used to promise never to drink any intoxicating drink. About the only boy that didn't come was almost the only one that was a strict teetotaller.

The village green used to be kept close-cropped as a lawn by the cows (about fourteen), kept by two small farmers, with no cars to worry them. The feast used to come once a year on 23 April and the green would be full of caravans and side shows, etc. This was village life in general for the working class family.

I remember my mother telling me that when she was a young woman, a Vicar of Thriplow, I think it was Revd Andrew, used to send his young daughters before breakfast to walk round the sheepfold, as every farmer then had a large flock of sheep. This was for health reasons as the belief was that the sheep's breath was good for them as there was a lot of consumption (TB) about then.

Working horses on the farms in the village were from eighty-five to one hundred (including Thriplow Heath Farm) and it was an interesting sight to see the farm men taking the horses out in the fields to plough, etc., sometimes as many as twenty, two or three to each man. A Mr Fordham farmed Cochrane's, Thriplow's and Duxford Grange farms and lived and farmed at Shelford. He had all his horses (eighty-five) on one big field at Thriplow at the same time, as he wanted to get it [the work] done quickly; a farm chap told me this. The horses' keepers had to get up at four in the morning to feed the horses before going to work then have their own breakfast, then have the horses ready for going to work at 6 a.m. in the summer and 7 a.m. in winter. The farm carts and wagons used to be painted in bright colours, blue bodies and red wheels.

And now about lark reeling (skylarks). In the winter when there was about two inches of snow and the birds couldn't get anything to eat, the farm chaps used to snare them with horse hairs tied about three inches apart as a noose on fine string pegged out in the fields in suitable places, and baited with oats, and go to them and take them out as they were caught. If he earned less than an ordinary day's pay (2s.) he had had a very poor day. They used to make about 6d. a dozen. I remember one winter in the early part of the First World War an uncle of mine caught forty-four dozen in one day and that made news in the *Daily Mail*. They used to be sent to London to hotels to be made into lark pies, a luxury then. Larks wasn't protected then as now. Now as you go over the paths in the fields one only sees an odd bird now and then. I expect that's what pesticide does. When the lark reels were repaired and put away for another winter they were well sprinkled with pepper to stop the spiders eating the horse hairs.

In March 1916 a blizzard blew up from the north and blew 200 trees down, mostly elms. No damage was done to any houses and as we looked out of the window it looked as if it was blowing along and not touching the ground.

The third decade started with a better outlook than the second (as wages were very low then). The war was over, masses out of work but the standard of living had improved a little and wages were a bit higher. One could hire the old cottage for 3s. 6d. a week which had no modern conveniences, a hole at the bottom of the garden for dirty water and rubbish that would decay. It was emptied when full to be dug in the garden. The unburnable rubbish one had to bury in the garden in a hole dug by yourself as the council didn't start to collect until the 1930s. If you had a thatched cottage it was nice and warm in the winter and cool in the summer. The cooking stove was the open type with cast-iron saucepans and tin kettles which were always sooty black. One could put the copper warming pan under and poke the hot cinders in to get a nice warm bed. There was a large garden to grow vegetables, a few chickens for the eggs and some had two pigs in a sty. In 1921 we got four new council houses which had a closed-in kitchen stove, three bedrooms but nothing else modern. They were empty for quite a while as not everyone could afford the 8s. a week rent. Water we got from open wells, some cottages had a pump. Twice the water table was low, most of the wells dried up and the farmers would bring the water round the village with a horse-drawn water cart. Some of the roads were still not very good but we gradually got from flintstones, that were thrown on loose and worn down by the farm carts, to the steam-rolled-in granite and finally to tarmac.

Farm wages were from 25s. to 30s. a week, skilled men (carpenters, bricklayers, etc.) 1s. 6d. an hour and their labourers 1s. an hour. These wages were kept like this for several years. Unemployment pay was only 11s. to 20s. a week. Farming changed a lot, horses gradually disappeared to make way for the tractor. In Thriplow there were eighty-five to one hundred which kept the blacksmith very busy. When he had shod a horse once he made a spare set of shoes for it. Sugar beet growing came in the early 1920s and was a slow job and hard work according to the present day's methods. Passenger transport improved in the twenties as well; from riding in the local carrier's cart, or walking to the railway station three miles away and into Cambridge, to going with Mr Softly, the sub-postmaster, in his Ford van, fare 2s. 6d, then to a kind of mini-bus with three steps at the back and curtains drawn across the back. Then came the motor bus and the Premier travel. The young people would cycle in on a Saturday afternoon, have a ham tea at the Three Tuns on Market Hill, then go to the theatre which cost 6d. up in the gallery. The caretaker would have cycle oil lamps lit for us then, with all our pocket money spent, we would cycle eight miles home singing on and off all the way. Motor bus outings gradually came along, single- or double-deckers with open tops. I remember going to Sandy Flower Show, in Bedfordshire, on the top of a double-decker and it was cold coming back at night. If some girls in domestic service worked in Cambridge they would cycle home on their afternoon off and back again at night. Some factories were being built in other villages and the boys used to cycle to work as there were only two motor cycles in the village and very few cars. Cricket or football matches on Saturdays were part of our recreation. Whist drives and dances were popular. Some of the lads used to go for a walk on a Sunday afternoon with one or two dogs catching rats in the farm hedgerows. In the winter evenings we would go for a drink at the Red Lion and have a sing-song. It was surprising how many songs the older men used to know as some of them didn't go to school after they were eleven years old. Children's games as I knew them in the first decade seem to have disappeared, such as marbles, spinning tops, hopscotch, skipping, running along with an iron hoop tapping it with a stick, rounders which I've been told is similar to American baseball.

A young man was well dressed with a blue serge suit, a bowler hat and trousers not too long to show a few inches of gaily coloured socks.

Tutankhamun's tomb was found in 1922, wireless broadcasting also in 1922, the first, and I hope the last, industrial General Strike in 1926. The first FA Cup match played at Wembley was in 1923 and the Wembley Exhibition was 1924 and '25. Colonel Fawcett, British explorer-missionary, went among the South-American Indians in 1925 and was never heard of again. The fashion for beards seems to have died out in the twenties. Two men told me they had never shaved in their lives. Some had a moustache but most were clean shaved. Hair was trimmed neat and tidy and there were very few who didn't wear a hat of some sort.

In the 1930s the farmers started ploughing deeper for growing sugar beet so when the airmen from Duxford were flying over they could see where the soil had been disturbed which one couldn't see when walking over it. This was in the 1950s. The farmers contacted the antiquarians who worked on the field all one winter, men and women. Bones, human and animal, and pieces of copper vessels were found. They was hoping to find the remains of Thrippa, a chieftain, but still, they proved that Thriplow was a settlement from 1000 BC, and how Thriplow got its name. That barrow was found in the field not far from the church.

CHAPTER FOUR

A BERKSHIRE BOY

*Life was tough for unwanted children in the early years of
the century as the experiences of Mr Herbert William
Edwards, who was left in a workhouse at the age of three,
clearly show. His native abilities and his determination to
overcome his early disadvantages are demonstrated in this
brief autobiography. His profound knowledge and love of
the countryside and of wildlife is evident in everything he
says. Though this essay has been transcribed from a series of
talks he recorded, his humour and ability as a story teller is
always evident.*

I was born on 18 October 1917 at Wootton Bassett.
When I was three years old my mother dumped me and
my elder brother in the workhouse. From then I was on
my own. I was sent to a children's home at Purton. At
the age of five I was sent to foster parents at Grove near
Wantage, where I was knocked about, and I was taken
from there in 1924, when I was six and placed in the care
of two old ladies who lived at Hampstead Norreys near
Newbury in Berkshire. They took in children like
myself for the money. I think they received 12s. 6d. a
week. There were two girls and myself, it was rough,
very rough, we had sufficient food but there was no

love and everything was austere and the discipline was very strong.

The cottage was two down: a sitting room, a kitchen and pantry. Upstairs there were two bedrooms. The two girls and the old ladies slept in one and I slept in the other. You had to go downstairs out the front door and round the house to the woodshed to go to the privy. There was no water laid on, you had to draw water from the well at the side of the house. There was an open fire with bars and a hob you could stand a kettle on. Later this was changed for a kitchen range, which was a great help.

We had to walk a mile and a half to school. It was a good school and took all ages from infants to leavers. We were lucky, we had a good schoolmaster. In class you could hear a pin drop, and God help you if the schoolmaster saw you were doing anything amiss out of school. We called him sir and the teachers miss. He was very dedicated and I think we learned more by the time we were fourteen than most learn now after they have been to college. We played cricket in the summer and football in the winter and there were seasonal games that children don't play now (they can't because the roads aren't safe). We played hoops and tops, and made bangers out of keys stuck to matches. We put a nail in, hit them against a wall and *bang* they went. Things weren't too bad, but I was treated as an inferior, all the children who were in these homes were treated as second class citizens.

I used to get up in the morning, run round the house to the privy, then I would take a bowl, dip it in the water-butt and wash outside, summer and winter. It didn't seem to do us much harm, but we weren't very clean. Then we had breakfast, mostly porridge and cocoa. We took lunch to school, there were no school meals in those days. Dinner was generally a home-cured bacon sandwich, which was nearly all fat. I didn't like that and used to take the fat out and just eat the bread. School started at nine o'clock and finished at twenty to four. In the winter, for 2d. a week you were given a cup of hot cocoa at dinner time.

On Wednesday we had an afternoon gardening, it was the only outside work we did at school. We looked forward to Thursday afternoons when we played football in winter and cricket in the summer. All the rest of the time was a steady grind. We had half an hour religious instruction every morning. We started with a hymn in the morning and finished with another before we broke up.

The School Attendance Officer came round every Friday afternoon. He went to see one family because their two children had not been to school one week in February. There had been floods and the water was deep. He got to the house and started to berate the woman. She said, 'How am I to get them through the water?'

'That's your problem' he replied, 'You have to get them to school.'

She asked, 'How did you get here?' and he had to admit that he had got a lift in a farmer's cart.

There was a big blousey lady with a voice like a fog horn that lived near the school. She used to scare me to death. There was an apple tree in her garden and the branches hung over the hedge on the side of the road.

Just inside the hedge there was this lovely red apple, I got on my hands and knees, hoping no one would see me, and I was just going to put my hand on the apple when her voice boomed out, 'I bet it's that Berty Edwards. I'll have your hide.' Good Lord Almighty I went along the road like a sprinter and into school to lose myself in the crowd but it was no good trying to hide for she knew who I was. She had a son whose name was Joe but she always called him Walter. On a Saturday morning she used to call him. 'Walter, Walter, your bath is ready', and after five more minutes, 'Joe, if you don't come and get your bath I'll have your ears off and I'll pickle you.'

From the age of ten I did a bit of work for a local farmer, feeding his chickens and so on. When I was twelve he told me to get an employment card so he could legally employ me, and in the holidays and at weekends I was working, but I wasn't allowed to keep the money I earned; the old ladies got that.

We had a bath on Saturday nights and that entailed getting water out of the well and getting it hot over the fire. The bath was put down in front of the fire then the old ladies bathed followed by the girls. By the time I got there you couldn't see the bottom of the bath the water was so dirty and it was also damn near cold.

By the time I was twelve I was driving horses and two-wheeled carts at harvest from the fields to the ricks. I left school at fourteen and went to work on the farm working with the horses, driving, carting and helping with other jobs. I was turned fifteen when the boss said, 'I want you to go in the cowshed'. They had eighty milkers (cows giving milk) and there were four of us to look after them. It involved starting work at five in the morning and working till five at night, except at harvest and haymaking when we were expected to help in the fields in the evenings. But before I go on to this I shall tell you about life in the village when I was a boy.

The village was a community of about three hundred souls. Every aspect of community life was very narrow and confined. The social scale was absolute and rigid. At the top was the squire, a titled landowner, he was the big boy, he controlled everything. Then there was the farmer who had Manor Farm and the other farmers who were slightly lower in the social scale than the squire. Next came the doctor, the parson and the schoolmaster in descending order. The cottagers were next but the lowest of the low were the gypsies, they were described as thieves and didicoys. It was said that the gypsy women would keep the housewives chattering at the cottage door while the men went round the back and pinched coal out of the coal shed. They would have anything. They were hated.

Then there was the village nurse, she was more or less one of us by virtue of the fact that she came into our houses. She brought all the kids into the world, she was health visitor, midwife and social worker rolled into one. There were two doctors, one had an old Morris 12 car with a dicky seat. His son used to drive him about. He told more tales than he cured people. There was no National Health Service then. The working class men paid into a Friendly Society, such as the Foresters, or into a Slate Club run at the pub. They paid 3d. or 6d. a week and that covered them if they were off sick and didn't get any pay from their employer. They got 9s. a week from the Slate Club and at Christmas any money left over was shared out equally irrespective of whether you'd had benefit or not. The Friendly Society was similar except that there was no Christmas share out. There was nothing against you being on the Slate Club and a member of the Friendly Society.

There was nothing for the women and children. If they were sick and had the doctor the man had to pay for them himself. That meant that they were at death's door before they sent for the doctor. There was one other very good scheme, if you made a voluntary contribution of 3d. a week to the local hospital the whole family got free treatment if any of them had to go into hospital. Everyone was frightened to be ill. The men had to pay 1s. 6d. a week (of which the employer paid ninepence) for National Insurance. If you received benefit you weren't allowed out after sunset. If you went out you lost your benefit, and there were informers. It shows how narrow people were, they would do down their own mates.

On the face of it the moral standards were very strict, if a lady hung a different pair of knickers on the line that was noted. If a courting couple jumped the gun and the girl became pregnant the banns were read in church within a couple of weeks. Further up the social scale the girl would disappear for a few months and then come back as if nothing had happened. A few years later the nipper would turn up.

Even in church we were segregated, the farmers and gentry sat at the front and we commoners got in at the back. The old parson used to preach like hell at us. Everybody had to keep their place. When the gentry or the farmers went by the boys doffed their caps and the girls curtsied.

Practically everybody in the village was Church of England but there was one family who was Roman Catholic and they used to bike all that way into Newbury to Mass every Sunday. We children did not like Sunday. We had to walk a mile and a half to Sunday school at ten o'clock. We came out at half past and went into church at eleven. The service lasted till ten minutes to twelve, then we had to walk home. At four o'clock we had to walk all the way back for the evening service.

It was a terrible crime to work on Sunday, except for looking after the stock. If a bloke was seen cleaning out his pig sty or digging his garden that was terrible. You didn't even dare to pick up a stick and take it home. Everybody put their best clothes on and walked about all solemn, and the more solemn ones were the most foul-mouthed on Monday morning.

The Church was determined to save our souls regardless of the state of their own. In a lot of cases their souls were in a worse state than ours, but they had the money to cover up their tracks.

Farmers and the gentry all had servants. They would take the cottagers' girls. A farmer might have three of his men's girls working in his house. They had to go to church. If there were three girls they would have one Sunday off in three. If there were only two they had alternative Sundays off. On the Sundays they were working they had to go to church in the morning and on the Sundays they were off they were expected to go to church in the evenings. These girls were up between six and half past in the morning and didn't finish till half past nine at night. It was a seven-day week for about five shillings, and that didn't go far even in those days.

There was no transport. If a bloke lost his job he had to find work within a radius of about seven miles, because when a man moved the farmer he went to was expected to send a carter with a wagon and horses to fetch his bits and pieces. If it was more than seven miles the farmer didn't want to know. If it was less than seven miles the word went round that he'd got the sack for something he did and the poor sod couldn't get a job anyway. There were no such things as written references, it was done privately. If a farmer wanted to know about a man he was thinking of hiring he would write a letter to his previous employer and get his opinion.

Farm workers' girls went into service and the boys went on the farm. Quite a few boys got fed up by the time they were eighteen and joined one of the services. Those that didn't break away stayed in the area all their lives and when a man's working life was over, in all fairness, the farmer didn't throw him out. I left school when I was fourteen at Christmas 1930 and started work on 1 January 1931. My first job was driving a dung cart. Three men filled the cart with four pronged diggers. There was a driver and one man out in the field. He pulled the muck out of the cart with a long-handled digger which had its prongs turned at right angles so he could pull the dung into heaps. Then a gang of men came along and spread the dung evenly over the ground. We worked from seven in the morning till four in the afternoon and for that I was paid 9s. a week. I had to give 8s. 6d. to the old ladies for my keep and kept 6d. for myself. I stayed with the old ladies until I went into the army.

The boss was known as 'Old Dad' but we didn't call him that to his face, the old men called him 'maister' and the young ones 'sir'.

Harnessing the horses ready for work was quite a job. To start with each horse had his own collar. That collar was made for that horse and it moulded into his chest muscles and became really comfortable. You put it on with the collar upside-down then you turned the collar the right way up and slid it down his neck. Then you took his mane out and settled it comfortably. Next you put the hames on, they were big brass things that stood up like horns. They were draped over the collar and tightened up at the bottom with a short chain. Then if a horse was what we called a 'filler', that is to say he was going to work between shafts, we put a cart pad on, which went where the saddle goes on a riding horse. Attached to this pad was a contraption of thick wide leather straps that dropped over the horse's hindquarters and were called breaches. The belt band was attached to this pad and tightened up. Then we slipped on the bridle and bit and we were ready to 'Shoot in'. Shooting in was the term for backing the horse between the shafts. There was a chain fitted to the shafts and once the horse was between them you threw the chain over the pad on the horse's back, slipped round under the horses neck and fixed the chain, at the right height to hook on to the shaft on the other side. On the hames there were short chains on each side called tugs that were fixed to hooks on the shafts. The breaching chain was fixed each side at the back then the only thing that remained to fix was the thick leather band. This went under the horse's belly and stopped the cart from going up in the air if it was loaded too heavily at the back. For heavy work we put a 'trace' horse in front of the 'filler'. This horse was harnessed with long chains fixed to the hames and a wooden bar was set to keep the chains apart, just clear of the horse's hind legs. You didn't need reins to drive these horses. If you wanted your horse to turn left you said 'cum here', to the right you said 'way out', 'whoa' to stop and 'go on' to start.

The art of harnessing work horses has gone now. The big shire horses had feet the size of dinner plates but they were as gentle as anything in this world if properly handled. They could work up some spirit at times and it was hell's own job stopping them from going along with the hounds when the hunt came by. In fact the carter used to shout to me, 'Hang on to him boy', and there was I about 3ft. 6in. high and weighing only 5 st., going up and down on the halter like an apple on a bell rope. If you could hang on it generally stopped them. One day one got away from me with disastrous results. I was working one horse with an artificial manure distributor. The hounds came by without warning at the moment I was filling the hopper, with the lines draped over the lever. The old horse decided he was going hunting as well, so away he went. There was an open 8ft gate through which the hounds had gone and he headed for it, I shut my eyes. He went through dead centre but the machine he was pulling was 10 ft. wide. What a crash! Duke was all right, he carried on with the two shafts hanging from his hames.

Hunting was a gentlemen's sport, and I reckon they lost more foxes than they caught. They sometimes caused considerable damage, for they would go through gates and not close them so that the cattle got out. One very foggy morning the boss said, 'I want you to go to Ramsworth' (a small farm within our big farm) 'There is thirty-five heifers there, but they've gone, I want you to go and find them and bring them back.' So away I go. You can easily lose yourself in a fog so you must stick to hedges or follow tracks. At last I picked up the tracks of the cows that led out to another farm and I followed them to a clump of yew trees. I thought, 'What am I going to find?' because yew is poisonous to animals, but there were no cows by the yews. So I continued along the track to a rickyard where I found ten of the cows still alive, the rest were lying there. I didn't know what to do. How was I to get these cows back the four miles to the farm. So I went to a farm nearby and asked the farmer if he would send someone to help me. He sent two men who helped me to get them home. Another time our cows got out into a field of kale and we had to tip the milk down the drain because too much kale taints the milk. These are aspects of the hunt that few people know about.

Just after the war we had a lot of heavy fogs and at that time I was looking after chickens in a very isolated place. There were woods nearby and as I shut the chickens up I heard pigeons 'lifting' up in the woods and thought to myself, 'there's somebody about'. I had my old shaggy dog with me and he had his ears up, I listened for five minutes and heard someone threshing about in the woods. So I shouted, 'Who's there, are you alright?'

And a fellow shouted, 'I'm bloody lost.'

I said, 'Stand still, and when I call you answer'.

A Berkshire Boy

I found him or anyway my dog took me to him. It transpired that he had been a beater for a shooting party. When they finished at four o'clock they told him to take a track that would save him four miles on his way home. In the fog he missed the track and he was still wandering about there at half past six, he was in a terrible state. I took him to my house, gave him a cup of tea, got out my van and ran him home. If I hadn't been there he would have had a night out in the fog because he hadn't a clue where he was.

Let me give you an idea of a working day in 1934 when I was seventeen. I was working the milking herd. My alarm went at twenty to five in the morning, I got up and dressed and had a couple of cups of tea from a thermos flask made overnight because I had no time to light a fire in the morning. I left the house at about five minutes to five, went to the pasture and drove the cows to the milking sheds. There were four cowmen, one went straight to the dairy to assemble the milking machines – there were four milking units. One went to the cowsheds opened the doors and lit the hurricane lamps, while two took the cows in.

Each cow went to her stall where her ration had been put out the night before. Her allowance according to her milk yield was in the manger. It consisted of linseed cake and oats. We went round and slipped chains on. You didn't lean over facing the cow's head when you put the chain on, you turned your back to the cow, put your right arm over and put the chain round the cow's neck behind the horns with your back to her so that she wouldn't hurt you. If you faced her and she threw up her head she would dong you in the face with her head or horns.

A cow has a lactation period of about ten months from calving to the end of milking. At the end of that time you dried her out and put her in the pasture for two months until she calved, then she was brought in again. . . . When a cow came in after calving she would go to the same stall that she had occupied last time, and it was hell's own job to make the silly thing understand when she had to go to another stall. However, after two mornings she was going to her new stall. Every time we had a new cow in we had to go through this ritual. Each cow had to be washed two times with lukewarm water, and as the man came round with the milking machine he would wash her again before putting on the machine. After she was milked by the machine we had to strip her by hand to get the last drop of milk. By the time milking was finished it was half past seven. In summer the cows were turned out to a grass pasture. In the winter they were turned out to a pasture where their food, consisting of hay or silage, mangels and kale, was already put out for them.

The men went in for breakfast at eight and by nine they were back on the job. They went back to the sheds and started getting out all the muck from the morning milking and they scrubbed everything down till it was spotless. All the water had to be carried by hand.

The bloke who worked in the dairy had to strip the machines down, the churns he was going to use in the afternoon would be put in the sterilizing chest at a temperature of 240 °F for twenty minutes. All the milking apparatus had to be sterilized twice a day. Rubber pipes were sterilized with boiling soda water, they came up like new. To cool the milk, before refrigerators, we had a cooler. Water from the well was pumped up into a holding tank and this passed through the cooler and was put out to the water troughs in the field. Milk had to be got down to 40 °F. In hot weather this was difficult and the milk could only be dribbled through the cooler slowly, taking a lot of time.

Cows with calves had to be fed and we had two bulls that had to be exercised. That was done by using a long pole with a spring hook on the end that went through the ring on the bull's nose, we also slipped a short rope round the bull's horns with two or three ropes knotted at the ends that hung down to ground level, so that if the bull knocked you down, or got away, he could not get very far off, very fast, for he would step on the dangling ropes and trip himself up or get so mad he'd either ram a tree or give up. He had to be exercised and watered, and while one fellow was exercising him the other would be cleaning his pen.

Then the calves had to be done. As soon as the calves were from six to eight week old they were taken away to an outlying farm and put in a yard where they were fed on cake until they were three months old, when, if it was spring or summer they went out to pasture, but if it was winter they stayed in the yard.

That took care of the morning till half past twelve when you got your dinner. At half past one you were out again to get the cows in for afternoon milking, when they also had to be groomed. There were three of us to groom eighty. You groomed them, you washed them, you milked them and then you turned them out and by the time you had finished it was five o'clock. To drive the milking machine we had a one-and-a-half-horsepower Lister 4 stroke engine. If it wouldn't start we had to milk by hand – it made your hands drop off!

We had to carry the milk five yards from the milking sheds to the dairy. The council used to run a clean milk competition and we won the cup three times in seven years but we never got a penny. The lady inspector used to drop in unexpectedly. Standards were very high then.

When the milking was finished a fellow came with a cart to fetch the milk and take it to the railway station; in dark weather he had a lamp on each side with a candle in it. There were two sizes of churn – a small one holding ten gallons and a large one holding seventeen. We used the smaller because they fitted under our milk cooler. They had two handles on the side and one across the lid which was fixed with a lead seal. A porter would get hold of a seventeen-gallon churn in each hand and run along the platform spinning these churns – no mean feat – I tried it and dropped the damn things.

We had to catch the five ten train that got to London by nine o'clock. There were trucks especially for milk on the end of the train. The station was a hive of activity as the porters got the churns, the crates of chickens and boxes to the right place on the platform.

At that time I was getting 17s. 6d. a week. When I reached twenty-one I got £2 2s. 6d. for a six and a half day week. I often put my hand in my pocket and found damn all there, but we had a packet of fags now and then and beer was 4d. a pint. You could get five Woodbine cigarettes in a paper packet for 2d. A week's grocery would come to 5s. for four. If a kid had a pair of boots they had to last, they were bought too big and he wore them till they pinched his toes. They were big hobnailed heavy boots. Children went about with their knees bandaged because they were always falling about with the great heavy boots on. I envied a boy who had shoes. In winter my feet were frozen in those boots. When it rained the water got in the top. Boys did not go into long trousers until they started work.

There was a windmill in the village and when I was a boy I used to love climbing on to the platform, the sails just missing my head. I would put my back to the rails lean back while holding on to the steel latticework and look upward past the sails at the clouds. You had the impression of going down at a tremendous rate, it was a wonderful sensation. It appeared that you were moving and the clouds were standing still.

When I was a lad nearly every cottage kept a pig. It kept them in bacon for most of the year and provided muck for the garden. It was a to do killing the pig. We arranged for the pig killer to come round and got straw ready. He got the pig out while we got hot water ready. The man killed and bled the pig. Then we laid the pig on the straw, heaped more straw round him and set fire to the straw. We went over him with sharp knives and took all the hair off and scrubbed him absolutely clean. We hung the pig up on a gantry and disembowled him, taking out the intestines cleaning them and putting them in water. We changed the water every day and turned the intestines inside out for a week, then they were knotted like sausages. We called them chitterlings and ate them fried. Then there was pluck – heart, liver and lights. We used to have every part of him. We loved liver and fry, but you can't get that now.

The pig was left hanging overnight. The pig killer would come back next day and 'joint up' the pig. He cut out the hams and the joints. We had brawn from the head, chops from the cheeks and fresh pig meat for weeks if the weather was cold. The sides were salted. We had a big trough with seams lined with pitch. We put a layer of salt all over the bottom of the trough and laid a side of pig on it and covered the pig with salt, laid the other side of pig on top and covered that with salt. Every day we swapped them round and rubbed fresh salt in. At the end of three weeks the bacon was salted enough to be cured. Then we slung the sides up between the beams and the ceiling, and when we wanted some bacon we got a side down and cut a slice off. The standard meal with bacon was potatoes and whatever root crop was going. Before Christmas it was turnips and after it was swedes, because swedes kept better. The whole lot was boiled, the bacon had to be soaked in water for forty-eight hours to get the salt out. It was a pretty basic diet.

Most farm workers had big gardens and they reckoned to grow enough potatoes to last them till potatoes came again. It was difficult to buy potatoes. You would have to go to the only farmer in the district who grew them. In their gardens they also grew brussel sprouts, winter cabbage, spring cabbage, savoys and broccoli, which they often planted between the rows of potatoes. They could always get turnips, swedes and kale from the farm. Old people always swore by turnip tops as a tonic.

Nearly every cottager had a chicken run with half a dozen or so hens and a cockerel. In the spring they would get a broody hen and put her on a clutch of about thirteen eggs in a nesting box. After twenty-one days the chicks would hatch. The hen was put in a coop while she had the chicks. They would get about six pullets and six cockerels out of a clutch. The pullets were kept for eggs and the cockerels were killed as soon as they grew big enough to eat. As the hens grew too old to lay eggs they were also killed and eaten, but they were tough and had to be boiled. The chickens were fed on household scraps mixed with meal. Nothing was wasted.

Farm Work

In spring we spent a lot of time sowing. We had three horses pulling a fourteen coulter drill (that is a drill for sowing corn that drilled fourteen rows at a time). The coulter tubes were about three inches apart. The drill was preceded by two horses pulling harrows that worked the land which had already been ploughed and prepared, then came the drill and this was followed by two more horses pulling harrows that helped to cover up the seed. You had to walk all day behind the harrow or drill. It was very tiring work.

In summer when the harvest was cut I would go carting; we used the scotch carts or wagons. The scotch carts had two wheels and the wagons four. There was a pitcher who pitched the sheaves from the shocks on to the carts, a loader and a driver who was usually a lad. When you got to the stack there was a fellow unloading and three on the rick. One was the rick builder, he was the boss man, and two to put the corn to him and fill up the middle of the stack. Each rick was built from the ground up, each layer three sheaves high. The first layer started with the butt of the sheaves pointing outwards. After two rounds the sheaves were reversed and placed with the ears outwards. You filled in to the middle and then started another layer and continued up to the top, which was either gable-ended or rounded. The rick was then left for the thatcher. Working steadily from seven in the morning till eight at night we reckoned we could put up a good rick. Ricks were about twelve yards by nine yards in size. You knocked off for an hour for lunch, half an hour for tea and worked till half past eight if the weather was good. If the dew was coming up and it was oats you were carrying you had to stop. If it was wheat you could carry on.

In autumn you were normally dung carting. We also had to pull and cut the tops off the mangel that were used for animal food, load them into carts and take them to the site where a clamp was being built; the clamps were many yards long and were covered. You had six day men (casual labourers employed by the day) pulling and cutting the tops off the mangel, and a team carting as with the corn.

Threshing was another autumn activity. You had a big threshing machine and an elevator. The whole thing was driven either by a steam-engine or a tractor. You had two fellows on the rick putting the sheaves to the thresher feeder who stood in front of the drum and fed the sheaves in; they had to be fed in evenly. There was no question of dropping them, they had to be put in quickly but carefully. A lad was on the left-hand side of the feeder, cutting the strings that bound the sheaves. He had to keep these strings and when he had a big bundle he tied them up and saved them for use during the year. Not even string was wasted.

The corn went through the drum on to the shakes that took it along. The corn and the chaff were separated by wind blown by fans. After the corn had been shaken out the sheaves were taken on and dropped on to the elevator which lifted them up on to the straw stack that was being built. There were two chaps taking the corn off in sacks and two carters taking the sacks of corn to where it was going to be stored. The tractor that drove the thresher was the only one on the farm in the early days and would have been no use for field work.

The corn was stored in a barn, but it was not clean enough for milling, malting or sowing, there was still one process needed to clean it and that was winnowing. The small machine used was known as a winnowing fan, it was made up of a holding box into which the corn was put, a rocker that could be regulated, and sieves of the appropriate size for the type of corn that was being worked. At one end was a big drum housing a fan, and the whole thing was worked by turning a handle. When you turned the handle the fan spun, everything rocked and shook, the corn dropped on to the sieve and into the wind created by the fan which blew all the rubbish and light corn out, and leaving beautifully clean even corn on the floor, which was then sacked and weighed. Generally this machine was worked by a team of three, with a boy to turn the handle. To old Albert nothing was ever right. He always used to moan about the speed of the thing.

Turning that machine was boring, and so sometimes the boy got into a gallop just for a change, Albert would holler out: 'Now you keep turning that regular boy, or else Old Dad'll be up here and he'll box your ears.'

Old Albert was the most bandy-legged man I ever saw. He had no hope at all of stopping a pig in a passage, but he always maintained, 'That be these here gaiters that make me look bandy. Why when I get them off my legs be as straight as any man's.' He used to ride a bicycle with solid rubber tyres. That was a rough ride on country roads, but he could boast that he never had a puncture. He used to get uptight if you referred to his tyres as solid. 'I tell you they baint be solid they be what is known as windless', he'd say. Most of the tools he used were long-handled. Albert always used to put the prongs of his fork through the carrier on his bone-shaker and tied the handle along the crossbar. He was riding down a steep rough lane one day when the string broke. The handle of the fork dropped and dug into the ground, and Albert who was riding at a fair old lick at the time was reared up by the prong stuck in his carrier then thrown all spead-eagled like a huge frog high in the air and yards ahead to land in a quickset hedge. I never heard language like that. He did go on!

Later he progressed to a pneumatic bike. He used to hang that on two hooks in his wood shed at night, 'Keep them tyres off the ground and they'll last,' he said. One night he went to his wood shed, lit a candle and spent some time chopping wood. When he'd done he went out, locking the door and forgetting the candle. Of course the thing he'd done wrong was placing the candle under one of the tyres of his new bike, some time later he could smell rubber burning. He profaned over that too. He didn't get a lot of luck not, to my mind, that he deserved it. As far as Albert was concerned it was as the Bishop remarked to the chorus girl when he saw the dog chasing the cat, 'There you are my dear, that is life for you, just one damn thing after the other.'

I was about fifteen when thermos flasks came into general use. Albert bought one in town on that Saturday afternoon and proudly brought it to work on Monday filled with cocoa. At ten o'clock everyone had a ten-minute break for nunchin. Ten minutes wasn't long enough to sit down and get comfortable so everybody ate their bit of food standing up. Now Albert proudly poured out a cup of cocoa all hot and placed his flask carefully on the ground beside the track and proceeded to walk up and down swinging his bandy legs well out and telling the blokes how it was good for them to have a nice hot drink instead of old cold tea. When he got level with his flask he did not notice it, kicked it over and smashed it. He almost certainly never bought another one.

The ten-minute nunchin breaks had to be worked off on Saturdays between twelve and one. Farmers were damned hard task masters. They were also very crafty and knowledgeable. A farmer who was blind was driven by his groom to a farm that was being sold. He made himself known to the selling farmer and asked to be taken on a short tour. Certainly he could. On the way round the selling farmer was extolling the virtues of his farm, when the blind farmer asked to be taken into a field, preferably a pasture. Once in the field he went down on his knees and felt about with both hands over the grass. He shuffled forward still on his knees, still feeling about. In a while he got up off of his knees, saying, 'No I shan't buy.' The selling farmer accepted with good grace, treated the blind farmer hospitably, but as the blind farmer settled himself in the pony trap to leave for home the selling farmer said, 'I respect your decision not to buy my farm, my friend, but what made you arrive at it, you only felt on top of the ground, that couldn't tell you how good or bad the soil was.' The blind farmer replied, 'I was feeling for thistles and there were none – and if your ground won't grow thistles, my friend, it damn well won't grow anything.'

There was a farmer who hated smoking. The workers nearly all smoked clay pipes, they were ha'penny a time and they smoked old black shag. The old farmer went into a field and found the carter smoking his old clay pipe, 'Carter,' the old farmer said, 'Tobacco ought to be a guinea an ounce.'

'That's a good idea,' said the carter with a beaming smile, 'especially if an ounce was as big as a hayrick.'

When I was looking after cattle we had two herds. One of about a hundred cows and the other of about eighty. Each cow had a name and I knew every one from both herds. One very hot day three of us had to go to an outlying pasture to bring home the cows that were near to calving. On the way home we passed a farm worker's cottage, and the man's wife called out, would we like a glass of wine, 'Oh yes, too true', we chorused. We knew of this lady's wine and how potent it was. It was good, it was sheer nectar. Well, the good lady poured out three tumblers full of three-year-old parsnip wine. Liquid dynamite it was, a lovely innocent-looking amber liquid. One fellow and myself sat quietly savouring it and appreciating the sheer elegance of the wine. But Frankie, the third man, was thirsty and he wurzelled it down. He drank it like a barbarian. Would we like a drop more, inquired the lady, 'Oh, yes please,' said Frankie. We others politely said, 'No, thank you. It's really lovely.' Frankie walloped his second tumbler down just like the first. We got a few cows together and went gently on our way. It didn't do to hurry the cows because of the heat and the fact that they were having calves. One particular animal didn't want to go on. She kept trying to break back and it fell to Frankie's lot to stop her each time. The further we travelled the more wobbly Frankie's legs became till eventually he sat down and said, 'I didn't know we had two moaners and both the stupid things keep trying to go back', we other two worked in closer and carried on to the home farm leaving Frankie sitting there cursing two moaners.

There was a village copper in every village. You never knew where he was. Crime was practically non-existent. The worst crime that was committed was riding your bike without lights. If you got caught and fined five bob what a mug you were! But there was one other offence that the policeman was looking out for and that was poaching. The village copper was trundling around his beat one night when he heard a gunshot in the wood he was approaching. He thought, 'Ah, a poacher, I'll wait and grab him.' So the constable waited at the end of the wood, along comes the poacher, pheasant in one hand and gun in the other. 'Got Yer,' says the copper.

'Fair cop,' says the poacher.

'Station for you, lad,' says the copper, 'come along.'

'I am stupid. I left my cap on the gate at the end of the wood. Will you hang on a minute while I run back and get it?'

'Oh all right,' says the law, 'but hurry up.'

About a year later the same copper was in the same place and again he heard a shot, 'It's that dratted poacher' he thought, 'I'll have him this time'. Sure enough along comes the poacher.

'Got yer,' says the law.

'Fair cop,' says the poacher.

'Station for you,' says the law.

Half a mile down the road the poacher stopped saying, 'Oh I am silly officer. Left my cap on the gate at the end of the wood, mind if I slip back and get it?'

'You had me like that last year, you must think I'm soft if I fall for that again,' says the copper. 'You wait here. I'll go and get it this time.'

Like most countrymen Mr Edwards was a keen observer and indeed a lover of nature, and he had many interesting observations to report.

You can see a lot of things in January. Take a walk across the fields and see the tracks where a fox has amused itself with a hare. The skidding marks of the hare as it turned sharply to get away, and the sudden stopping of the fox with his tracks going almost straight back. The fox doesn't turn like the hare, but goes up in the air and turns as it comes down. I said amuse itself, for foxes don't often kill hares, they are not partial to them. Look under elm, beech and oak trees and see where the birds have scratched in the leaves for nuts and acorns. When the sun shines, watch the trees for grey squirrels basking. Look for their tails hanging down, it always gives them away.

February is what I call a moving month when everything starts to grow. There is an old saying, 'Where the wind blows on Candlemas Day (2 February) there it will blow till the 2nd of May.' Elder is the first tree to sprout and the small leaves look amazingly like a mouse's ear. Snowdrops and celandines bloom and St Valentine's Day is said to be the birds' wedding day. Rooks and partridges have already paired off and one thrush had two eggs by 14 February this year, which reminds me of a story. Mr Blackbird got home and found a strange egg in the nest. He asked Mrs Blackbird, who said, 'I did it for a lark'. It is also a ploughing month. We used single furrow ploughs drawn by three horses, the first horse led by a boy. One boy hated that job, he prayed for rain. He was standing by the stable door one morning cursing the ploughing when suddenly he shouted, 'Carter, carter, it's raining in the pond.' The carter answered, 'We ain't going to plough in the pond, boy.'

March brings, 'breezes loud and shrill that stirs the dancing daffodil'. It is the time for mad hares and storm-cocks. From late February through March into April the buck hares endlessly chase the does, jumping and kicking and running in and out of places they avoid all the rest of the year. I once saw two hares run through a cow shed while we were milking. There is a curious thing about hares – they can't see directly in front. If you see a hare coming straight towards you stand still and it will keep on coming until a few yards away when it will get your scent. Then it will check, turn its head a little, see you and away it goes.

I've seen storm-cocks, a gale blowing and bitterly cold, perched on the highest tree around, with easily six feet of travel in the wind, whistling gloriously. On and on and on, to and fro in the gale. The end of the month brings daisies to the lawn but it won't be spring till you can cover twelve at once with your foot. This is the month for drilling corn. Years ago they used to broadcast the corn, but it was a bit wasteful, because wild birds and pigeons particularly could easily pick up the grains from the ground, but when the corn is drilled it is in the ground about two inches deep. The birds still find some, but not to the same extent. We used to have days at pigeon shooting and there were lots of days when I shot over a hundred. My highest tally was 255. They were then, and still are, a great pest and need to be kept within reasonable limits. I like casserole pigeon. It's about the only thing I'd leave home for.

Crows are dull black birds with black beaks and whiskers. They usually forage in pairs, a cock and a hen. They never mix with other birds and live on carrion. Now when the sun shines on a rook he has a purplish sheen on his back, and a grey beak. Rooks are community birds living and nesting in flocks. The funny thing about them is, that although they live in flocks they mate for life. They don't often eat carrion. The buzzard is like a very large rook but with a shorter more fan-like tail and rounded wings. He is as ugly as sin and is protected by law.

If you hear a rabbit squealing don't run to the sound. Have patience until all is quiet then go to the place. The rabbit will be quite dead, the stoat will run away on your approach and you have rabbit pie on the stoat.

During the war I went home on leave, it was late autumn and dark when I arrived. There was very little food in those days and I took half a dozen rabbit snares to set out in a field beyond the village, intending to be up early the next morning and collect what I had caught, so no one would know. I set my snares, there was just a sliver of moonshine and I went back to the village across a stubble field. I heard a rustle in front of me and after a couple of strides I saw this old rabbit stop. (A rabbit stop is a short hole in the ground which a rabbit has made to have her young). Ah, I thought, she's gone in to that stop. So I dropped to my knees and shoved my hand up the hole to grab the rabbit. I pulled it out like lightning with a flaming great rat on my thumb. I gave a yelp, shook it off and away it went. During the next week, back in the army, my thumb went very sore and septic and I had to report sick. The MO looked at it, lanced it and mucked about with it and then said, 'How did you get it?'

I said, 'I was erecting barbed wire, sir, and there was a tear in my glove.'

'Funny,' he said, 'If it wasn't so improbable I should have said you were bitten by a ferret or a rat.'

Pheasants don't pair up. The cock bird wanders about getting a group of eight to ten henbirds. He mates with them all and each hen selects a site and makes her own nest. She then lays ten to fourteen eggs and when she is ready to sit she neatly lays feathers taken from her breast in between each egg. If you see a nest that is not feathered you know that she is still laying. The cocks will fight almost to the death when they are collecting their harems, that is why most gamekeepers have a cocks only shoot at the end of the season, to get the numbers down and eliminate cock fighting. A hen pheasant is a bad mother. If she is out with ten chicks and it pours with rain she will keep going on as long as she has got one chick with her.

Partridges are different, they pair and the hen bird goes and lays an egg each day. Each time she lays an egg she covers it until she has finished laying. Partridge keepers carry a cane and with this cane they can feel in likely looking heaps of leaves to find the eggs. The Partridge uncovers her eggs to sit and does not use any feathers for cushions. She is a wonderful mother and often rears every one of her sixteen to eighteen eggs.

The plover uses a small hole in the ground and places half a dozen small twigs in the bottom and lays two or three eggs. You will never see a plover alight near or arise from her nest. When going to it she alights a fair distance away and casually wanders to it. Similarly on taking flight she will walk a distance before taking wing. The skylark does exactly the same. When horses were used for all arable work the carters watched out for plovers' nests and when they came in the way of the work in hand, the carter would move the eggs out of the way and replace them the next time around. Plovers are very respected by farmers, but in these days of huge tractors the drivers can't see the eggs and many get destroyed. The skylarks fare much better for they usually nest in pastures which at that time of year are usually left alone and grazing animals never seem to interfere with nests. The male plover is very aggressive to other birds at that time of year. He will rise and screech and dive-bomb any bird that is flying near his sitting mate. I have seen them drive off hawks and crows, and if a cock pheasant happens to wander anywhere near there is a row. I saw a plover rise one day and fly off, you could almost hear him grunting with the effort of getting up speed, and for the life of me I couldn't see what the panic was, so I watched him and he suddenly took on a hawk almost half a mile away. What eyesight he had!

Plovers and partridges, when they have young, feign injury or make the most distressing noises should anyone go near their nests. The idea is that the interloper will follow them or try to catch them, and all the time the intruder is being lured further away from the young. Once the distance is considered sufficient the 'wounded' bird makes a miraculous recovery and flies off.

One of the prettiest sights is that of a moorhen with a brood of very young chicks. They follow mum in a single file and look like a lot of black bumble-bees – their legs are so tiny they just seem to float along.

Country folk get a feel for the weather and can usually foretell it better than the weather men. Here are some signs. When the leaves of the aspen, the silver birch and the lime turn up their tips, it will rain. When the rooks by mad flying high, wide and handsome making baskets in the sky – rough wet weather is in the offing. When you see pigs dashing with straws in their mouths rain is close. When the sun is suddenly brilliant and the shadows black and sharply clear get to shelter for rain will be on you in minutes. When blue mist hangs in the trees and the hills are distant and hazy it will be dry and hot. When everything dries quickly or white frost goes off quickly and everything looks close and clear it will rain. When swallows are but specks in the sky, when the skylarks descend as slowly as they went up, still singing, the day will be glorious. If the new moon is lying on her back, she is holding the rain in her lap and it will be a dry moon. If she is standing up it will be a wet moon.

Weather is important when ferreting and the phase of the moon is expected to affect the behaviour of the rabbits. When ferreting, go quietly to the warren, clear the bushes away and fix the nets over the exit holes and slip the ferret in. When the moon is waxing the rabbits will bolt and get caught in the nets, except in wet weather, on the other hand they will not bolt if the moon is waning.

If St Swithun's day is fine there will be no rain for forty days but if it rains on that day it will be wet for forty days. This must be taken within the context, as must all weather sayings, for if the day is wet but falls within a dry spell, or if the day is dry and falls within a wet spell then the saying does not work. There is another saying about Candlemas day – if the day is bright the winter will return but if it is dull the winter is over. It is also said that if the ice in November will bear a duck the rest of the winter will be wet and muck. If animals lie down in a group or young animals run about with their tails up, there will be thunder.

CHAPTER FIVE

A CHESHIRE
CHILDHOOD

The stark realism of Mr Albert Owen's life story provides an antidote to the nostalgic approach of many other writers on life between the wars.

I was born Albert Owen on the 23 June 1916 into a world of suffering, sorrow and poverty, just about a fortnight before the Battle of the Somme, during the war in which my mother's two brothers, like many others, suffered horribly. My father was exempt because he was a farm worker, so I was born at Iddenshall Hall cottages just a mile or so on the Chester side of Tarporley. I started school at five and left at fourteen. I went to about seven little schools in that time, just ordinary elementary Church of England schools. I had two brothers and four sisters. They went to other schools after I left. We got used to father coming home after an argument with his boss, for it usually meant an upheaval and removal, for the farmer always had the last word which usually was, 'I shall want the cottage'. If you said 'Boo' you were sacked, turned out of the house, and faced with having to go to the workhouse. The tied cottage was the curse of the times, the farmers knew the workers couldn't find another job and treated them awfully.

All this moving meant leaving school friends and meeting new ones, learning new lessons and new ways and starting all over again. Some schools you liked, some you didn't and it was the same with the teachers. You'd just get settled in then it was off we'd go again.

Every Friday night there was a rush to the newsagents for the *Chester Chronicle* and father would scan the 'Sit vac' columns for farm workers which were quite long in those days. You avoided the farmer who advertised regularly for he was no good. I knew one who advertised almost every fortnight. The advert was always the same. 'Good worker, wife to milk when required' which meant if he beckoned his finger when the cows were in full flush in the spring she had to turn out eight or ten cows morning and night, and then come home and get the children to school. When the worker's son left school, if he'd any size about him, the boss demanded him to work for him as cheap labour. The worker and the horse had a lot in common, both were over worked and under rewarded. Often the tied cottages weren't fit to live in, and as a result there was a lot of sickness. But there was no Health Service then so you had to pay the doctor.

Of course this meant you never sent for the doctor if you could help it. This was where home remedies and herbs came in. I remember my dad nearly losing his arm through blood poisoning. My mother had no sleep for a week, but she saved him through poultices, just before he was to go to hospital to have his arm off. In her tiredness she upset a saucepan of porridge down her legs, but she had to carry on with badly scalded legs. When dad found a suitable job advertised he'd borrow a bike or walk if it was not too far. If it was a good farm he'd probably find half a dozen men in the yard before him. This was what the farmer revelled in. He knew he had them in the palm of his hand.

If father was successful he'd give his notice, and the following week he'd rise early, walk to his new job, get the horse and lorry ready and bring it to where mum was waiting, having packed our few goods and chattels. The old sofa was placed at the front of the lorry for us kids to ride on. The rest was piled on behind. At the back would be the empty rain tub – an old treacle barrel from the farm – this would have half a dozen hens in and a roll of wire netting ready for a hen run in our new home.

It was just too bad if it was a wet day, the biggest problem was keeping the bedding dry. It was a day's job, arriving about dusk or just after depending on the distance and the pace of the horse. We'd be all night getting the beds up, and food on the shelves, for dad would have to start work at six or half past next morning. Mother would be worn out. Next morning we'd spend exploring and finding our way about, and we'd wonder how long it would be before we'd be off again, depending on the tempers of my father and the farmer.

My happiest memories were of Alvanley school, I left once but came back again. I had more friends there. My main pal was the son of father's boss who lived up the road from us. So all my playtimes were spent with him up at their farm. We had good times playing round the haystacks and buildings, helping at harvest time, setting and getting potatoes, ricking hay and fetching cows up from the fields for milking. We used to get a big yard brush and sweep the cobbled yard at weekends for which we used to get a penny or twopence which I kept in my pill box money-box on the mantel-shelf. Many's the time when mum had gone milking I'd turn my box upside-down and insert a broad knife in the slot hoping to get a copper for the sweet shop. It was rare if we got sweets, all money was spent on clothes and shoes.

This time of year (summer) was marble time and top time; we used to play top all the way to school. There were two kinds of top, one was pear shaped. We used to colour the top so it would look nice as it spun round. The other type was mushroom shaped. These were called 'window breakers' and if you had a good whip you could do just that with them. We played marbles along the gutters. We used clay marbles; if you hit your mate's marble that was yours, we hoped to get a multi-coloured glass alley but we couldn't afford to buy one of those.

Another game was called peggy. A peggy was a short piece of stick pointed at both ends like a pencil. You hit it 'tiddly-wink' fashion with another piece of stick (a piece of broom handle was ideal). As you hit one point of the peggy it would jump in the air, then you hit it again. The furthest hit was the winner.

Winter was hoop or trundle time. The village smith would make one for ninepence, but mum couldn't afford that so I'd to play with someone else's.

Springtime we'd be in the wood or down the lanes bird-nesting or gathering wild flowers for mum. I always knew where to find the robin's nest in the hedge; behind the ivy leaves, lined with horse hair and wool. I always knew where to go for the big king cups or the shaking grass which was lovely stuff. It used to tremble and shake as you held it.

One time I went with another lad whose hobby was budding roses on to a wild rose with a bit of clay and raffia. Sadly he died at the age of fourteen from meningitis. I remember they carpeted the road outside his house with straw, as was the custom to deaden the noise of the farm carts. They took me to see him in his coffin. I wish I'd never gone, I still remember it. He still lies in Alvanley churchyard.

Another game was playing boats down the stream. We'd throw a piece of stick in upstream and follow it down and the first home was the winner. Happy days!

The school had three rooms. There were long desks and forms with three ink wells in each. Of course you were not allowed pen and ink until you could write properly. You weren't allowed to speak or make a noise and anyone who misbehaved would be placed on the mantel-shelf, a big broad old-fashioned thing. Mr Harniman used to pick you up and put you there, you daren't move or you'd fall off. I remember him well, he always had a white waxed moustache and a red rose in his button hole which had a little silver phial behind full of water to keep it fresh. The sons of farmers and the well-to-do sat at the front of the class next to the fire and also had extra tuition after hours. The peasants sat near the door in the draught, and believe me it was bad in the winter. The Christmas party was the highlight of winter. There was a real fir tree nearly up to the ceiling with real little coloured candles. It was in semi-darkness so that it showed up beautifully. We played games and had presents of fruit. I remember seeing a little barrel of grapes. I didn't know what they were, having never seen or tasted any before and I was seven or eight then.

Another spring pastime was looking for coot's nests around the pits. They always nested well away from the side. If we couldn't reach them we'd go home for a big spoon, tie it to a long stick and ladle the eggs out that way. Then we'd light a little fire and boil them in a tin, lovely! These pits also provided good sliding places when frozen over in winter.

We always had half a day off for Empire Day on 24 May which was known to the boys as 'legging down' day or 'nettling' day, when we chased after the girls nettling their legs.

We made all our own fun, we'd no toys, only what we made, and a pair of old socks, past darning, was our football. Crossed clothes pegs were our cows and horses. We were in bed by seven or half past and if we were hungry we got a slice of turnip or carrot dipped in salt.

We had plenty of religious instruction in school, first we said grace, then prayers followed by reading the Bible for an hour, then grace before we went to lunch and also after lunch, and a hymn before we went home, usually 'Now the day is over'. We were taught respect, manners and tidiness, sadly lacking today. We were even taught to know right from wrong. Our homes were poor. Dad only got about 35 s. a week for seven days' work. Stock had to be attended to night and morning. He had a bit of time off on Sunday between ten o'clock and four.

We had no modern conveniences such as electric light, water, bathroom or modern sanitation. The waste water ran from a drain under the house into an open ditch across the road. We carried our drinking water in a bucket from the farm pump. I had to go in my dinner hour for half a bucket, all I could carry. The farm was five or six hundred yards away. The rain tub provided other water. We had a wash house across the yard with a bake oven in it. We hadn't many clothes: one set of best clothes, no underclothes, just a jersey and trousers, weekday and Sunday. A pair of clogs lined with rushes or wheat straw which kept our feet warm and dry. I've seen mother banging her head on the wall with toothache because she couldn't afford to go to the dentist. They were hard times but us kids were happy having known nothing different.

It was a hard life on the farm, all the work was done by hand or by horse, with long hours in the field. I've seen my dad's hands full of deep sore cracks after pulling mangolds or cutting kale on frosty winter days. He'd rub vaseline in them at night. My mother was a champion milker in her day. A good milker was valued by the farmer. She kept the milk streaming into the bucket with a nice steady movement. If a person had nice comfortable hands the cow would let the milk down easily as she ate her corn. The boss always followed the milkers in what was known as 'stripping'. After waiting ten minutes or more he could get a few more squirts out – if there was more the milker got told off. Of course no one had the same kind of hands. A rough person could find himself kicked off the stool, so a kicking strap was placed above the cow's hocks, threaded through a loop to form a figure eight. This saved spilt milk and upset milkmen. Milk was an important part of the income. The monthly milk cheque was very important as there were no subsidies as there are today. I have seen half-dead TB cows still having their milk taken off them. I've seen cats fall into the vat of milk when they had been mistakenly locked in the dairy all night, but the milk was still used. A lot of Cheshire farmers made cheese all summer, a hard, trying job but butter and cheese added to their income. The whey and butter milk were fed to the pigs (I'd love some butter milk now).

Arable crops were grown mainly to support the livestock. Oats were grown mainly for the horses along with mangolds and turnips which were put into clamps to last through the winter. Every Saturday morning the old gas engine would be chugging away grinding oats. Roots would be wheeled out of the clamp to be diced like chips and mixed, by hand, on the barn floor. The meal didn't come ready mixed as it does today, so everyone mixed their own taking the components out of a hopper that had separate compartments for bran, India meal, thirds [wheat offal] and barley or fish meal. It was hard work. In the stable it was the same. The hay was kept in the loft above, and the hay was chopped by hand for mixing with oats and bran, for working horses need feeding. It was a nice feeling on a winter's evening when you had fed, watered and bedded them down for the night, to leave them contentedly chomping away at the hay. As you left and turned out the hurricane lamp they would turn and whinny. I used to think they were saying 'thank you'. A lot of clover was grown in those days, now its all silage and some kind of rye grass. It was lovely looking over the field gate at a good standing crop with pink and white clover flowers and broad leaves. I always picked a bunch to take home for mother's hens, she used to hang it on the wire netting. The eggs were rich with an orange colour. The hens were running loose on the farm and were more of a sideline for the farmer's wife. There were no batteries or cages.

Pigs and poultry always seemed to make for one place to root and scratch; no one has ever found out what they got out of the ground. If they had, they would have made a lot of money. Springtime was the time for setting broody hens, thirteen eggs to a sitting. Sometimes they would be given duck or turkey eggs to hatch.

Corn from the mill would be delivered by the old Sentinel Steam Wagon. You could bet it was always dark and you'd be busy milking when they came. This time of the year was particularly busy. You were praying for dry weather, for cultivating and breaking the soil for planting spuds; for drilling and getting the muck into the drills. Two persons carrying a box between them would walk up the drills dropping the sets in. Afterwards they had to be covered up – all back-aching work. Then there was the spring oats to be sown and rolled in. All this was done by hand and horse and you were ready for bed at nine o'clock, for you had walked miles up and down during the day.

Farmers were more particular then, children would be employed picking large stones off the fields and throwing them in gateways, and the corners of fields were dug out with a shovel and sown by hand so no inch of ground was wasted. When the young oats got a few inches high men went up and down the rows with a paddle; a stick with an inch blade on the end chopping the thistles before they got too big, for there is nothing more painful than setting up stooks of corn that are full of thistles.

Hedges were cut by hand and ditches and watercourses cleaned out and the mud plastered on the banks. Work was done properly or you were out of a job. Now it's all rush, profit and greed, tractors and chemicals, much to the detriment of people's health.

The biggest change in farming today is freedom from poverty and the tied cottage, and the change over from horses to tractor, for some of the horses were treated cruelly and some were turned out after a hard day's work without as much as a rub down with a wisp of straw or a feed.

I followed the threshing machine for a year or two, that way I had more money and Sunday off. My parents never had a holiday, I never had one myself till after the war. But the farmer always had his and plenty of food. I remember the grocer being told off for bringing the groceries during the evening milking and exposing the good food and dinner wine to the workers. They never went short like the men. I remember my parent's evening meal in summer, just stewed rhubarb and bread and marge. Not much in that for a hard day's harvesting. Up early at five every morning, four in the summer, and working till dusk. Just after the war a neighbour had his first holiday, a week at Blackpool. He got home for dinner on the Saturday and rushed to do the evening's milking scared to death of being late and getting a cursing. Yes, the farmers were 'bastards'. Sorry, but I can't think of any other description.

I shall conclude with two verses written by my uncle, T. Wilton, a champion ploughman who died a few years ago aged eight-four.

The Breake-Me

I rubbed your nose and stroked your mane
Then unsuspecting down the lane
You followed one, you'd been before
You'd recognize the stable door
You knew these trips would always lead
To oats and bran, a tasty feed.
Well that was how the scheme began
To break you to the use of man.
An end to all your coltish ways
In shafts and chains you'll end your days.
Don't let that rankle in your breast
Perhaps some day they'll let you rest.
And anyway you're not the first
To be bamboozled and coerced.
Don't feel ashamed it's nothing new
For I was broken just like you.

Wake Me

Wake me at four its flaming June
With Lark and Thrush I'll be in tune
When meadows lie with mist adrift

To be a Farmer's Boy

And o'er the meadow wheels the swift.
Wake me ? – But no – not quite so soon
Forget it – let me sleep till noon.

T. Walton, farm worker

Carting hay. An old reaping machine is in the background. (Mr R.W. Hawkins, Manea, Cambridgeshire)

A steam-driven threshing machine at work. The straw is being passed up the elevator on to the stack behind the machine. (Mr R.W. Hawkins, Manea, Cambridgeshire)

Loading up the hay cart. (Mrs M. Poole, Ipswich, Suffolk)

*These men are gathering the sheaves and standing them up to dry in shocks,
usually consisting of eight sheaves. (Mr L. Wallis, Rochester, Kent)*

The shepherd. (Mrs M. Poole, Ipswich, Suffolk)

A group of farm workers in the 1920s. (Mr M. Hewins, Farnham, Surrey)

A pair of horses in full dress for a show.
(Mr C.F. Barker, Stowmarket, Suffolk)

Turning the plough. (Mr L. Wallis, Rochester, Kent)

Putting hay into the loft. (Mr L. Wallis, Rochester, Kent)

A wagoner at work. (Mrs M. Poole, Ipswich, Suffolk)

Taking the horses to water, 1935. (Mr F.L. Goldsmith, Bedford)

Mr Sheppard's team in the 1930's – Dodman, Captain, Poppy, Smart, Club and Ruby. (Mr L.J. Sheppard, Trimley St Mary, Ipswich)

Muck carting in 1932. (Mr L.J. Sheppard, Trimley St Mary, Ipswich)

A reaper-binder at work in 1936. (Mr L. Maw, Selby, Yorkshire)

Mr F. Goldsmith driving a Fordson tractor in the late 1930s (Mr F.L. Goldsmith, Bedford)

Workers with a corn drill in 1944. (Mr L. Maw, Selby, Yorkshire)

Boys help to load sacks of corn on to the lorry that will take them to the mill.
(Mr L. Wallis, Rochester, Kent)

Cutting the corn with a self-binder

Tractor-drawn machinery at work; in the foreground rib rolling, in the background sowing fertilizers. (Mr L.J. Sheppard, Trimley St Mary, Ipswich)

Planting potatoes. Two men – one sitting on each side of the machine dropped a potato when the bell rang. This was a great improvement on hand planting. (Mr L.J. Sheppard, Trimley St Mary, Ipswich)

CHAPTER SIX

NORTHUMBERLAND STORY

Mr Robert Fortune told us:

I was born on 5 October 1906 at Brock Hill. My father was an estate carter on the Hammerstone Estate about seven miles south of Berwick-upon-Tweed, on the mainland opposite Holy Island. My mother was a shepherd's daughter. I am now retired. I was a farm worker until I was sixty years old and then I got a job as a gardener for the last five years. I had two brothers older than me and two who were younger.

When I was four years old I remember seeing Haggerstone Hall being burnt down. I was standing at our door and could see flames coming out of the windows about a mile away. We then moved to a neighbouring estate, Lowlyn. Not so large as the Haggerstone estate. The grass fields were let off to farmers. My father's job was to keep the fences in order, repair gates, cut hedges, look after the woods and also the water supply. This was pumped up to a large water tank by a windmill then fed to the various places on the estate by gravitation. His wages were 19s. 6d. per week plus firewood which he had to cut by hand. The house went with the job. We kept a pig, some hens and a goat, and we also had a good piece of land where we grew potatoes and vegetables. The goat used to graze on the roadsides. I was five years old then and ready for school. It was a church school. We started the morning by singing a hymn, then we had an hour's religious education by the vicar. We had four and a half miles to walk to school, wet or dry. The village, Lowick, had another school and several shops. Having older brothers I had to wear a lot of their cast off clothing.

At Christmas it was the custom to buy the teachers a Christmas gift. One year the boys bought a goose for the man and a duck for the woman. They were both alive. When the teachers came in the morning they were told, before they went in, that their presents were in the school, but they had to catch them first. They chased the duck and goose round the classroom while the kids watched through the windows. My school days were happy enough. I used to go fishing in the stream with a long stick and a line and some worms. There were loads of trout in the burn. I had some good catches, but I never ate them – the rest of the family did. In the holidays I went round with the rat catcher who showed me how to set snares. After a while he gave me six snares for myself on condition that if I caught more than two I was to give him the extra ones.

By 1914 Haggerstone Castle had been rebuilt and during the war it was turned into a military hospital. Then I was taken very ill, the doctor came and inserted tubes into me, there was no anaesthetic and the pain was beyond endurance. For two weeks he came every other day to clean the tubes, a very painful operation. Then one day he took the tubes out and he did not come back. The nurses at Haggerstone hospital heard that I was very ill so two nurses came every day washed me and brushed my hair. I was living on nothing but milk. When I felt stronger they used to bring me light food. When the time came for me to get up I could not walk. One nurse got at one side, the other on the other side and helped me. After I recovered I went back to school. One year after I had been taken ill my parents got the doctor's bill. It was for £6. They had a struggle to find the money. At the finish they got enough and I was sent to the doctor's to pay it. He asked me who I was, when I told him he said, 'I never expected to see you again.' When the estate changed hands my father had to leave. The houses were all the same. They had a large fireplace with a wash pot on one side and an oven on the other and cement floors. The toilets, or netties as they were called, were outside along with the coal houses and ashpits. No council dustmen in those days. A bath had to be taken in the back kitchen with water heated in the kettle or washpot.

The wives would wash on Monday with a barrel and poss stick, starting to heat the water as soon as the husband went to work. Thursday was baking day, the dough was set beside the fire to rise with the yeast. My mother used to bake seventeen loaves besides scones. There was no transport so one could not go shopping. The groceries came each month. The Co-Op and Walter Wilsons stores had travellers who came on their bikes and took the orders for the month's supply. The groceries came a few days later, delivered by a horse and float. There was no tinned stuff in those days.

The wives did all the knitting and made all their men's shirts. A draper used to come round on his bike with a pack of shirting material and wool.

Money was not plentiful. The wives generally got the man's pay and paid all the bills. They would not get anything unless they could pay for it, there was no credit.

On winter nights rug-making started. A newly made rug was often put on the bed for warmth. The lighting used was paraffin lamps and candles when you went to bed. Meals were cooked on the open fire, anything special in the oven. Steam pans were used, potatoes in the bottom, vegetables in the top. Soup was usually made in a hanging pot. The fires were made with a bar up the chimney with an adjusting hook to hang pans on.

A butcher used to come once a week with a horse and van from the nearest village. The farm workers always had plenty of ham and bacon because everyone kept a pig or two. The pigs were generally killed in the months between November and April. A well-cured pig would keep for a year. All the farm cottages had hooks in the ceiling to hang the bacon on. That bacon had a taste of its own far better than the stuff that is sold now!

I left school at the age of fourteen. I was not hired, but the farmer took me on as he had a contract for carting at a girls' school. My wage was 2s. a day. I had to get up at five o'clock in the morning to feed the horse and get it ready for starting work at six o'clock. I had to help with the milking, then harness the horse, yoke the cart and deliver the milk and potatoes to the girls' school. That took until eight o'clock when I had twenty minutes for breakfast. Then, if there was no more carting to be done, I worked on the farm, picking stones off the fields, planting potatoes, singling turnips, cutting thistles, worked at haymaking or corn harvesting, helped the farmer with the sheep or fed the cattle.

In autumn, after the corn had been cut with the horse-drawn binders the sheaves were stooked, eight sheaves to a stook, four on each side holding each other up. This was the method of drying the corn, with the stooks stood up in line with the prevailing wind. The stooks stood in this position until the corn was ripe and dry (hard). Then they were led (taken) to the stackyard in a horse and long cart (a special cart for the purpose). There would be people in the field to fork the sheaves up to the driver of the cart, who would then drive it to the man who was building the stack. Each man who stacked the corn had two or three carts bringing corn to the stack. The number of carts used depended on the distance from the field to the stackyard, (the greater the distance the more carts, so that a constant supply of corn was reaching the stacker). The last load was taken to the back door of the farmhouse, with all the workers riding on the top of the load. There they would receive a drink of beer to celebrate the finish of harvest. The stacks were covered on top with wheat straw held on by ropes made from oat straw.

The potatoes were taken up when the children were on holiday. The older children would be taken on by the farmer to pick the potatoes. This was the time when the farm worker got his potatoes. He would make a potato pit or clamp in his garden, keeping some to use.

Turnips were pulled, topped and tailed and put into pits covered with straw to keep the frost out. These were used as winter feed for the cattle and sheep. Sometimes turnips were heaped in the field, five carts loads to a heap, for fattening hoggets [young sheep]. A hand cutter was used to cut turnips and someone was employed to do this as the animals got fed two times a day. They used to put the cut turnips into baskets to use at weekends.

The cattle courts [sheds] had to be cleaned out and the manure put on the fields before the ploughing could be done. During the winter the ploughing was done. Cattle were brought in to fatten, and the sheep had to be fed.

Some farms had a built-in thresher for threshing the corn. This was a job for the bad weather, when the land was not fit to go on, but a travelling thresher was hired when a lot of corn was needed. It was driven by a traction engine that took about thirteen workers. The smaller farms worked together. The neighbours sent their men when there was threshing to do.

In spring we finished off the ploughing, and when it was wet we dressed the corn for seed with a hand-turned dresser, sorted potatoes for seed by hand or made straw ropes for thatching corn stacks, again by hand, one man feeding the straw in, the other doing the twisting with a throw-crook as it was called.

Seed corn was sown with a fiddle. The man walking and keeping in step with his arm using the bow. There was also a corn server who carried the corn to him when his fiddle was empty. The rest of the workers would be harrowing the seed in.

When summer came there were turnips to be singled, but the main event was haymaking. When cut the hay was left for three or four days to dry, then it was kyled, that is to say made into small haycocks. The small kyles were gathered together with a hay sweep into a pike or large haycock. After the hay had been in the pike for a week or more it was led home on a hay bogie where it was built into stacks.

With regard to the relationship between master and man, that is a difficult question, it depended on who your boss was. If he was a gentleman farmer – that is, if he had enough cash so that he did not have to work – I would say the relationship was that of master–servant. With regard to the working farmer, who had not so much cash, well some of them one did not think much of. Others were friendly but they were all alike in one way. They all liked their pennyworth. If they gave you anything they expected double back.

CHAPTER SEVEN

A NORFOLK COUNTRYMAN

Mr G.W. Coleman, who was eighty-seven years of age when he wrote this account, lives at Wymondham in Norfolk.

When I was twelve years old in 1912, I picked stones on the fields in winter when the fields were bare. The stones were used for roadmending. Men sat on stone heaps using a hammer to break the stones. They had gauze to protect their eyes. Mr Tom Kiddle did this work near my home. I worked for Mr John Dring who was the farmer of Park Farm Wymondham. We received 6d. per day and were promised 1d. extra for the boy who picked the most stones. I gave 3d. to the Primitive Methodist Chapel and was led to believe that I was pleasing God.

When I started work in 1913, after schooldays were over, at Ivy Holme Farm Silfield, I received 3s. 6d. for a sixty-hour week. In 1914 when men on each farm bargained for harvest wages I had £1 (the first one pound note my father or I had ever seen since they were first brought into being in that year). We did a month harvesting, filling out time on other jobs during the wet weather or after the grain was all harvested, but there was no Sunday harvesting then.

My father's name was in *Kelly's Directory* for 1900, the year I was born, for he was a boot and shoe manufacturer, having a one-man business. His shop had five spare seats and local workmen would come and enjoy sitting together and talking. Most of them could not read and a young man would bring in a newspaper and read the biggest of lies. The topic one evening was about the way time changes as we travel round the world. One man said that solved a mystery that had puzzled him. One day his master had sent him to Hethel, which was about half an hour's journey, with a horse and cart. The men at Hethel were starting their meal saying it was twelve noon. When he arrived home his mates were just starting their meal also saying it was twelve o'clock.

I remember my father leaving off work to look at the first self-binder, cutting corn and tying it in sheaves. In those days (about 1910) some of the farmers had their barley cut with scythes and turned with forks before carting it loose for stacking. Grain was stacked near the gate into the fields where it grew, and a cumbersome steam-engine brought a drum for threshing and an elevator for conveying the straw up on the stack. Sheldrakes of Bunwell were owners of threshing tackle, as it was called, and so was Bob Flint of Morley St Botolph.

My father-in-law, Jack Andrews of Hardingham, used to walk from his home to Acle with cattle that spent the summer on the marshes. They travelled home by train looked after by Charlie Wymer who was aged about sixteen. There were hedges and gates to all fields then which were smaller than they are today.

A tale I heard in my father's workshop was about a smallholder named Fred Bunn who bought a horse at Spelman's sale at Norwich. A boy asked if he could take it home for Fred to Silfield about ten miles away. So Fred gave the boy a note to give to Fred's mother saying, 'Please give this lad 4 shillings'. The boy changed this to 14 shillings. The poor old lady thought it a lot to give him when wages for a man were about twelve shillings a week, but she paid.

When I was at school from 1904 to 1913 we used to see farm wagons each Michaelmas day conveying furniture, with women and children moving into new tied cottages, for at that time of the year men changed employers for a variety of reasons. One man told me he had to move because his wife always quarrelled with the neighbours. In some of the tied cottages you had to share the shed containing the copper for washing and the lavatory with your neighbours. In 1922 I lodged with Billy Steward at Ryburgh, he shared a toilet with two other neighbours.

I left the farm to work on the railway in 1917 but have always lived among farm workers. As I finished my early duty on the railway at 1.30 p.m. I was asked by small farmers to help them, and during the Second World War I spent my holidays at agricultural holiday camp.

When working in the fields, farm workers tied sacks around their legs for warmth and protection from rain and snow and they also fastened a sack round their shoulders for a cape. One day when Mr Eke was burning hedge cuttings his sacks became very dry and caught alight and he died. My most amusing story was of Poley and Clarence who bargained to work at Gateley Manor, about three miles away, starting at 5 a.m. for 5s. a day. Clarence said to Poley, 'If I'm late one morning tell the steward I've got a puncture in my back wheel near the Rectory and stopped to mend it', Clarence was half an hour late on the first morning and told the tale, but the steward said, 'Poley is not here yet'. So they both got the sack before they started.

On a cold morning men would say, 'There's a good steward on duty this morning', meaning that they would have to work hard to keep themselves warm. When cutting grain by hand one man was appointed 'Lord' and the others followed.

Men often worked alone especially on small farms and were happy to have a horse with them pulling a cart or implement, and many were very sad when horses were replaced by tractors. One chapel preacher told his congregation that if an ox or an ass fell into a pit on the Sabbath day they would pull it out because otherwise they would have to buy one to take its place. My father made whole-tongued boots for farm workers for there were no rubber boots in my school days. He charged a week's wages but they lasted for ten or twelve years. When they were worn out he would use the uppers for wooden clogs.

Mr Stimpson of Fulmodeston hired a second farm and offered his head horseman a job as steward living in the farmhouse. The new steward put a lock on the granary door because the men, unknown to the farmer, would take corn, which they should not have done, because they wanted their horses to look well. When the lock was on the horseman made a hole in the floor to let some corn from the heap, then put a cork in to conceal the hole. When the farmer went to the granary the heap of oats was like a funnel in the middle.

Men who made corn stacks would trim the eaves and any loose straws at the side of the stacks, especially if the stacks were near roads. On Sundays during harvest they would walk round looking at each other's stacks for they were very critical of each other's work. When the corn was ready to harvest they would take a few ears from each field to make corn dollies.

In those days men took pride in their work. When they were carting manure to the fields and making small heaps to be spread with a fork they placed these heaps the same distance apart counting their footsteps.

Dick Joice's father (Dick Joice is a well-known Norfolk broadcaster) had four farms near Ryburgh where I was employed from 1921 to 1929 and he would allow his men to have a day off and take their wives and children to Wells-Next-The-Sea. The horse brasses were polished in the men's own time and the gay ribbons tied on their manes and tails. Billy Steward was team man with three others for John Savory of Highfield Farm, Great Ryburgh. Billy went to work about 5 a.m. to feed the horses, taking his breakfast and made toast on a little oil stove. He started work with the horses at 7 a.m. His wife used to fill a glass bottle with tea made from the leaves left in the pot after we had our cups of tea each evening, and Mrs Nelson next door filled another bottle for him which he warmed on his oil stove adding milk produced on the farm. He was a good man giving generously to the Salvation Army instead of spending on himself. One of the team men went at 9 p.m. each evening to look at the horses when they were in the stable. One night a horse was on the floor with its head tangled in the rope on its halter. The rope had a block of wood attached to the other end. Horses would scratch their foreheads with a front foot and it was assumed that its foot went on the wrong side of the rope. It had to be destroyed. The horses lived on the meadows in the summer and one man, taking turns, would look after the horses on Sundays.

A horse belonging to Ernie Pleasants fell into a drain with only its head and neck visible. I phoned for the fire brigade who got it out with difficulty using slings and a tractor, but it had to be destroyed. He also had some fat cattle grazing with the horse and lost one. It was assumed it had completely disappeared down a drain.

I am very sad when I think of the devoted and dedicated farm workers shedding tears when the horses they loved and cared for were sold and replaced with tractors.

It was quite an event when a mare had a foal on a farm. If a mare was expecting twins it usually had a miscarriage, but I knew one mare that reared two foals. I have seen some strange animals. I once saw a stuffed foal which only had two forelegs, a calf with two heads whose mother had to be destroyed, and a lamb with six legs. I once saw a ewe sheep on its back with a lamb bleating near it. If a sheep gets on its back it cannot get up. I pulled the ewe to its feet and the lamb looked up at me and baaed.

We have had sheep conveyed by rail counted in at the start of a journey, and at the destination more counted out – some being born on the journey. Animals do not like being taken from their young. A cow belonging to Mr Savory was taken from its calf and brought to Ryburgh station to be conveyed by rail. It badly injured one man and nearly injured me. It rushed about jumping fences and was rescued by bringing a few more cows to calm it down.

Horses were sometimes used to drive the elevator conveying straw or sheaves of corn to a stack; not many horses liked that job so the mare that would do the job was called the willing horse. Horses were sometimes used to tow railway wagons and those that refused were called jibbers. I would attach the horse to a wagon on a falling gradient, take the brake off and it would start to pull the horse back. Some men had very cruel ways with horses such as placing a thorny piece of stick from a blackberry bush under its tail, and if a horse laid down refusing to get up and work they would light a little fire near it.

Men working in the open would take a midday meal with them. When working what was known as a 'One journey', that is to say two four-hour shifts, they would take a few old newspapers or a bunch of straw and light a fire with sticks taken from the hedge to make a camp fire, and bake a potato or two in the hot ashes. My wife would give a cup of tea to such men, as we lived at the crossroads, so they would have their meal near our house.

Farmer Savory was conveniently deaf at times. He took a sample of barley to Smith's Maltings asking 30s.

a comb for it but Mr Smith started bidding lower and said 29s. 6d. was the highest he would give. So Savory started riding away. Smith shouted to him to stop whereupon Savory said, 'Thirty bob, right, I'll send it tomorrow'. [A comb was an old measure of corn, it was equal to 4 bushels, that is to say 32 Gallons or approximately 145.25 litres.]

One day I was working on a stack infested with mice and rats and a mouse ran up my leg although I was wearing cycling clips. One man had a rat run up his leg and ever after he tied a piece of string round his trouser legs if he was not wearing high-topped boots.

In my young days before wireless or television young men found pleasure in destroying sparrows, catching them in a sieve on a pole. They would take a dog and prod the rats out of the stacks. Farmers would pay ½d. a tail and after paying them one farmer would throw the tails on a manure heap from which the impoverished rat catchers would retrieve them to resell them to the farmer. This farmer left 2s. in the stable to test the honesty of his men, going in each day to see if the shillings were still there. One Saturday they were missing so he asked the team man where they were. He was told they were, 'On the muck heap with the rest of the S . . .'. The workers were amused to see the farmer retrieving his money.

Many heaps were turned over regularly and some farmers would bury an iron harrow so that they could tell if all the manure had been turned over properly or not.

Men saved money to buy a good watch and carried it in a small pocket on the top of their trousers. They had quite a performance finding it when they were wearing their protective garments (sacks).

I have mixed with many types of workers and if asked for the most trustworthy and honest men I would say, 'The sons of the soil'.

CHAPTER EIGHT

A NORFOLK CHILDHOOD

Mr James Mann of Clenchwarton, King's Lynn. From the broad flat acres of west Norfolk we received this detailed account of a happy childhood. It is particularly interesting in that the writer describes his experience of life in the home and enables us to see from a child's point of view the life of a country wife and mother.

I was born on 24 March at Clenchwarton. At that time births took place at home. A village woman was sent for. She assisted at many of the births and also laid out the dead. She was not a qualified midwife.

Some babies were kept in long clothes for several months. The mothers usually breast fed their babies for many months. The babies were weaned on bread and sop, potatoes mashed in gravy, rusks and so on. In a lot of households the first outing a mother made was to the church to be churched.

My present job is in a potato packing factory but by trade I am a blacksmith having served a seven-year apprenticeship. My first job on leaving school was as a milkman for a local dairyman. He had his own cows and in 1944 he supplied most of the village and I used to do my rounds on a tricycle. The milk used to be measured out in pints and halves into jugs on the doorstep.

I had a happy childhood, we didn't have much money but never wanted for food or clothes. My father grew our vegetables and mother made the clothes, she was always knitting something. She used to cook on the kitchen range. We had one tap over the big sink. No electric light – we had paraffin lamps and an old-fashioned flat iron.

Wash day was on a Monday. We always used soft water for washing. On wash day my mother was always up early, the copper had to be filled from the well the night before and the fire to be laid under the copper. The copper was a large metal vessel set in a brick framework, the fire was under the copper. All this was out in the shed. In the morning all she had to do was put a match to the paper. If the wind was in the right direction the water was hot in an hour or so.

The clothes were set in place around the kitchen floor, the whites to be washed first in a large metal bath. They were rubbed with knuckles on a scrub-board. When washed the whites were put in the copper to boil again. It took twenty minutes or so, then they were removed with a wooden stick into the copper lid to allow most of the water to run back into the copper, for hot water was not to be wasted. The whites were put through the mangle then rinsed in cold water. The rinse water and the hot water from washing the whites was then used to wash the dirty clothes. The whites were 'blued', mangled, then those that needed it were starched and put on a pile. If the children were at home they did the rinsing and mangling, a cold job on a cold day. After hanging out the clothes on the line we finished up with 'hot aches' in our hands. Frosty weather was good for the linen, it made it softer, so it was hung out on even the coldest days. There was a race between the women to be the first to get their whites out on the line. Some went so far as to cheat by doing the whites the night before. Wash day was busy and Monday tea was usually the remains of Sunday's roast.

If the washing got dry, ironing was usually done on Tuesday. We used flat irons. These were heated in the black-leaded stove, one being heated while the other was used. The skill was not to over-heat the iron. This was tested by spitting on the face of the iron, or rubbing the iron over a piece of old cloth. They always had to be rubbed anyway because they got black from the stove. If you forgot to rub them they could put a black mark on your best tablecloth. Too hot and you could scorch the shirts, too cold and the cotton would not press, just right and they would work like a dream. The starched things had to be ironed damp and the artificial silk underwear had to be ironed with a cool iron and with very great care. The ironing was done on a wooden kitchen table which was covered with a few layers of old blankets kept for this purpose. The linen was then hung on lines slung across the kitchen. We then spent the next two days trying not to knock them off as we walked across the kitchen. It was a good thing the washing was only done one day a week. My mother took great pride in white washing. A modern washing machine would have had a hard job to come up to her high standard.

We children had to bike three miles to the village school and later seven miles to the secondary school at Terrington St Clement. The weather had to be very bad or the road blocked before we were allowed to miss school, if we could only get through on foot it was on with the wellies and we walked. The junior school had three classes, infants, middle and top. All the classrooms were heated with coal fires and if you sat at the back on a cold day you shook and could hardly hold your pencil, particularly if you had got wet on the journey to school.

In the top class a child was often asked to run an errand for the headmaster, sometimes this was to take a note, to help his wife fold the sheets, to weed his garden or to roll the village cricket pitch for the weekend match. We also had a day when we would go round the village on a salvage drive for the war effort, collecting old pots and pans, tyres, paper and anything that could be used for the war effort. The school was visited by the mobile dentist; we did not enjoy his visits. Another visitor was the man who tested our gas masks, we did not enjoy that one either, in those hard gas masks we felt as though we were choking. We did like trips out in the autumn to pick the rose-hips that grew in the lane around the school; they were sent away.

We took a packed lunch until the senior school had a canteen built, we then had it sent to our school in metal containers that kept the food hot. It was a great day when the first school dinner arrived.

The games we played were energetic and rough and tumble. The winter game was football. In summer we played cricket. The playground games were tag and skipping. In tag you ran about the playground and on being caught, or tagged, you joined hands with the person who caught you till eventually there were as many as twenty joined together. The girls' main game was skipping, sometimes the boys joined in as well, this we did singly or in groups. For this a child was at each end of the rope and a child would jump in to skip. Sometimes we played 'bumps'. This is to turn the rope twice or more but only jump once. Sometimes a hundred or more bumps could be done one after the other. We also played high jump. In the summer we played ball games and 'two ball' was popular. This was a series of various ways of throwing two balls at a wall and catching them. The better players used three or even four balls in the air at the same time. In another game a player faced a wall with closed eyes. The other players lined up some way off. The aim was to touch the player by the wall without him seeing any of the other players moving. If he turned but saw no movement he had to turn back to the wall, but anyone he saw moving would have to go back to the start. You could either rush and risk it or creep along and risk being caught with a leg in mid-stride. Station was another game. To play this we drew a lot of circles in the dust. A catcher was chosen. He had to try and catch the runner before he could reach a station. In the station you were safe.

At times the headmaster was a right old tyrant but we respected him and his cane which he frequently used. Discipline at school was character forming and made us respect our elders and other people, and made us better citizens in later life. At home when we had no chores to do we had the run of the farm. We were not allowed to walk on the crops but could go round the headlands and through the grass fields. We wandered and played games of imagination such as cowboys and indians. The boys always being the cowboys and the girls the indians. We played houses. Making the houses in the tall grass, standing sheaves of corn for rooms and passageways. We made tree houses with planks and sacks. We climbed all the trees that were climbable and in summer we sat in the leafy trees and read a book. We had lots of fun round the two farm ponds and numerous drains and dikes. We dipped for small pond life, we went stirring for sticklebacks and fishing for newts and water beetles. We knew where every bird built its nest, how many eggs were in the nest and how they were coloured and marked. How exciting it was when the eggs hatched out. We taught ourselves to swim in the deeper of the two farm ponds. This was unknown to our parents for we had been told to stay away from the pond, but of course water draws children like a magnet. When the water froze over we made slides on the ice. Once my sister fell through the ice and was lucky to get out, of course mother wasn't very pleased when she came home soaked through and freezing cold.

We ran bare-foot when we could get away with it. We were wild and free and happy with loving parents. We never went on holiday, except perhaps once a year on August bank holiday, when we would go to Hunstanton for the day, this was a great treat.

The cottage we lived in was quite old, probably the original farmhouse which at some time had been divided into two cottages. The other cottage was unoccupied. Ours had three bedrooms: one large with a fireplace, one medium and one small. These had sloping ceilings and small dormer windows. Steep steps led to a front door which was never used. Downstairs there was a large front room which was only used on 'high days and holidays'. It contained a very large table that had belonged to my father's father and it could seat sixteen people. During the war it was my sister's and my air raid shelter. When the sirens sounded mother would make us get out of our beds and sleep under the table. I never felt afraid when under that table no matter how loud the bombs sounded. That room also contained a suite of furniture consisting of two arm chairs, a couch and six dining chairs all leatherette covered. By the window was a treadle sewing-machine which was my grandmother's. A tiny cosy kitchen was the room where everything was done. This had a range where a kettle always sang and a large black pot of water always stood. There was a large bread oven which no longer worked and which was used as a storage cupboard. There was a wooden table, four chairs and my father's wooden armchair. When he came home anyone who was using it got up and let him have it. Mother used it when he was out. The kitchen floor was of quarry tiles covered with newspaper and lino with a hearthrug near the fire.

Everything was done on the kitchen table, all the cooking from meat preparation to pastry making and vegetable peeling, so it was frequently scrubbed. All the washing-up, ironing and sewing was done on the table. We all sat round the table to eat. Sometimes different members of the family were doing different things at the same time on the table; mum washing up, dad working, a child doing a puzzle, with a pile of linen waiting to be ironed. Two steps led down to the dark little scullery which had a brick floor and a slatted window with no glass. Outside was the coal house and the shed.

Our parents had a feather mattress on their iron-framed bedstead. It had fancy brass knobs at head and foot. We children had iron bedsteads with flock mattresses. My sister had a patchwork quilt all beautifully sown in herringbone stitch that had been made by our grandmother. We all had washstands with a jug and basin in our bedrooms, but these were never used. We used to wash on the kitchen table. We also had pots under the bed, these were used, for it was a long cold trek in the middle of the night to visit the outside loo.

The toilet was an earth closet in the garden. It was a hole in the ground covered by a wooden seat, this included a high seat with a large hole for the adults and a low seat with a small hole for the children. The paper was squares of newspaper hung on a string on the door. As a child I was always afraid of falling down the hole and never stayed long. In the dark winter evenings I hated walking down the path with a quivering candle, which usually blew out leaving me frightened in the dark. I only went when really necessary. At times the hole needed to be emptied, my father did this. A large hole was dug in the garden and the 'night soil' was bucketed in. It was not a pleasant job.

My mother cooked all our meals – there were no convenience meals in those days. We roasted in the oven of the kitchen range. Kettles and saucepans could be heated on the top of the range. We also had two Primus stoves, used for boiling and frying when the fire was not lit in the range.

For breakfast we always had something cooked; bacon, sausages, eggs, fried potatoes and so on. This was followed by toast done on a fork before the fire and spread with beef or pork dripping. Nothing tasted like it. If there was no fire, bread and jam or marmalade filled the odd corners. If it was a cold morning we were told by father to 'fill our boilers up to keep out the cold'. In the winter we sometimes had porridge.

Our lunch, we called it dinner, was usually eaten out of the house. My father took a packed lunch, usually bread, cheese and an onion. No neat sandwiches, but in chunks which he cut with his knife. This was washed down with a bottle of cold tea, until he got a flask. We children took a packed lunch to school, jam, cheese or meat sandwiches. If we were at home we had toast and dripping.

Our evening meal, tea, was always cooked. We all sat down together unless it was harvest time. We had a roast twice a week Sundays and Wednesdays. With this we had Yorkshire pudding and beautiful gravy. This was followed by a sweet of some kind, fruit pies, apple dumplings, spotted dick, rice pudding, stewed fruit, jam roly-poly and so on.

The rest of the week we had boiled meat, stews, casseroles, puddings and pies, with these we had a lot of fresh vegetables in season grown in our large garden. In late winter when most of the stored vegetables were used up we ate dried peas and beans. On Saturdays we occasionally had fish. We ate nothing fancy but had good wholesome solid food. We kept chickens so we usually had eggs. My father worked hard in the garden so we had fresh vegetables. Fruit was grown on the farm so we usually had apples, plums, pears and damsons. We collected wild berries and seeds, elderberries, blackberries and mushrooms in the fields. We could find the eggs of wild birds such as moorhens, pheasants, and partridges. We sometimes got a rabbit or hare, strawberries and raspberries in season and samphire.

Bread and milk was delivered to the door. When the weather was bad and the vans could not get through the supplies were left at a farm a mile down the road. It had to be bad for this to happen.

For a year or two the only water supply we had was from the well in the yard so we all had to learn to draw water as soon as we were large enough to pull the full bucket up on the rope. This was not easy as the nearer the bucket got to the surface of the water the heavier it became. Lifting it up the last few clear feet took a lot of pulling and some wells were quite deep. One method of drawing water was to have a tight hold of the end of the rope and drop the bucket upside down into the water. If the air was not knocked out of the bucket it would not sink. Then the bucket had to be jiggled at the end of the rope to make it sink. The best way was to lower the bucket to very near the surface of the water, then with a flick of the wrist turn the bucket into the water. If this was done properly the bucket would sink first time. If one was really careless the rope slipped through your hands and the bucket and rope sank to the bottom of the well. This always seemed to happen when we needed water in a hurry. We then had to fish for the bucket with a long-handled crome, a fork with a bent tine. You would hook the bucket and rope and pull it to the surface only to see it slip to the bottom when you tried to lift it clear of the water. Every so often the well was cleaned and emptied. The walls were scrubbed up and the sludge cleared from the bottom. My father did this until I was old enough to do it. Our well had a leach in it. These were said to keep the water clean. I remember the water tasted good – really cool on a hot summer's day. When the well ran dry we got the water from the village water cart. This went round all the outlying farms because nearly everyone down the Marsh had to rely on wells and water butts. When the army took over the farm during the war they put in a supply of piped water, although the tap was across the yard about a hundred yards away we thought we were in the lap of luxury. They also brought the telephone to the big house and we were allowed to use this in an emergency.

Bath time came at most once a week. A long tin bath was taken from its place in the shed where it hung on a nail. It was put on the hearth rug in the kitchen. The towel was hung to warm up over the fire guard, the soap was put on the floor. Steaming water was brought from the copper to the bath and cold water added. The youngest was bathed first. Then after our hair was washed and rinsed in cold water we were wrapped up in a warm towel while the next child was bathed and so on through the family. A screen was placed round the bath when we got older. It was a real treat to get out of the warm bath and dry by the fire, and after a cup of hot cocoa to be taken to a bed heated with a hot water bottle. Sometimes after her hair was washed my mother would put my sister's hair up in rags – these were long cotton strips. The hair was divided into sections and each section was wrapped around a rag and the rag wrapped round the hair and tied off at the bottom. She looked very funny. In the morning when it was taken out – hey presto – ringlets. Most of the time my sister used to have her hair in two plaited pigtails tied with ribbons. The worst chore of bath night was emptying the bath. It took two persons to carry it outside and empty out the water. As we had no drains it was emptied on the grass. As we children got older we had to empty the bath ourselves.

Another treat was the radio, it ran on a big dry battery and an accumulator which could be recharged. This always seemed to run out during the most exciting part of *Dick Barton* or *Children's Hour* which we always listened to. The accumulator had to be taken to the town to be recharged. We usually had one in use and one on charge. As the power soon ran out we were not allowed to listen all day. My father always listened to the six o'clock and nine o'clock news especially during the war. Most radio shops used to collect and deliver the accumulators on a regular basis like the milkmen and the bakers. We never had electricity in our cottage but it did come to the village three miles away. Soon after the war the better off people began to get television and we would gaze in wonder as the aerials began to grow on the chimneys. We never thought that one day we would have one of those. I think that the day the queen was crowned there was about six television sets in Clenchwarton.

My father was a horseman and there were five horses on the farm. He got up at about 5 a.m. His first job was to give the horses their feed, then he came in for his own breakfast, then he went back to get his team brushed and harnessed up for the day's work. The type of harness used depended upon the type of work the horse had to do. If the work involved pulling carts they wore heavy collars and saddles.

One of the first things I learned was how to harness a horse. If they were pulling a light harrow their collars and chains, locally known as traces, would be all that was necessary. Father made his own lead lines and could do up their tails and manes with ribbons. This was done on very rare occasions as it took so long. He understood horses very well and the horses seemed to understand him. They had a good working relationship.

In the autumn and winter wagon loads of potatoes were taken to the railway station six miles away. I sometimes went with him and, depending on the load, three or four horses were used to pull the wagon. Though only nine or ten years old, I was never allowed to ride on the wagon when it was loaded, my father said the horses had enough to do to pull the wagon when it was loaded. I was allowed to ride home, sometimes on the horse, but usually in the wagon. I loved the bump and roll of the metal-rimmed wheels on the road and the steady clop of the horses' hoofs, with my father talking softly to his team. It was so peaceful.

Sometimes I went with him when he was ploughing. He could plough a straight furrow, the horse carefully placing its feet in the furrow. He let me try one day, the plough jumped and jiggled, I found it very difficult but he said I had them going very well, this was praise indeed. It was always said that a normal day's ploughing with a single furrow plough was about one acre, that was equal to walking fifteen miles. In the harvest we boys were sometimes allowed to drive the loaded carts back to the stackyard and take the empty carts back to the field to be loaded again. Our legs were not long enough to straddle the horse's back so we tried sitting side-saddle, we soon got used to the roll of the horse's walk but the rub of their coats against our legs made them very sore. All boys in those days wore short trousers until they left school at fourteen. At the end of the day the horses were unharnessed, rubbed down and fed before my father would think of changing his own wet coat.

Usually, when the men had their meals the horses were given a nosebag containing oats and bran, or corn and bran thus allowing them to feed at the same time as the men. Often the men referred to dinner time as 'dockey time or nosebag time'. After their feed the horses were watered.

Father would go to the field in the morning and call his horses up, only on very rare occasions did they fail to come. In the spring it was the case of catching the mare and leading her in, then all the other horses would follow. Sometimes I was allowed to give them their oats, which was stored in a large wooden bin. To reach the oats, when it was getting low, I had to tip myself right inside the bin and hang on for dear life while I scooped up the oats in a metal bowl. Then I had to push between two huge (compared with me) horses to tip the food into their feed trough. They would nuzzle their soft noses in the grain and snort out the chaff. If two horses leant together as they fed it was a tight squeeze to get out.

Later on father went tractor driving. It was easier work but he didn't find it as satisfying, he never sang to his tractor. Most early tractor drivers were ex-horsemen.

If we could get a load of wood we spent hours under a starry sky sawing this into logs with a large cross-cut saw, father at one end and either my sister or myself at the other. It was hard satisfying work and we sang or talked as we worked. It was all worthwhile when we saw a pile of warmth-giving logs stored in the shed. My father said sawing wood was the first of two warms, the second was when you burnt the logs on the fire.

It was an exciting time for us children when the threshing tackle arrived. The tackle consisted of a steam-engine, a drum, an elevator, a chaff cutter and some-times a baler. It was pulled into the yard where the stacks stood like huge round tents with thatched lids on top. Threshing was usually a winter job, though it was sometimes done during harvest time. If I was on holiday my job was to fetch the water for the engine. The engine had an insatiable appetite for water.

I used to have a tumbril for the coal and a three-wheeled cart for the water, which I had to fill up with a hand pump. The old wooden door on the water cart wasn't a good fit and by the time I got back to the engine half the water had gone. The driver would put his suction pipe in and with one big slurp the water all went, so I had the whole process to do again. In between this I was fetching coal and looking after the chaff and all for the sum of £1 a week.

The engine had a fascination for me. It was a mass of moving parts, pistons, cranks, rods, wheels. All the brasswork was shining. It smoked and wheezed like a friendly dragon, and that special smell of a steam-engine still has a fascination for me. The driver always had a dirty face and hands, and oil-smeared clothes, his cap must have been held together with oil and grease, it seemed to shine. He always had an oil rag in his hand. The large flywheel which took the belt that drove the machines had a special interest. I could never understand why or how the belt kept on. If you didn't duck low enough when you were going under the moving belt it made a nasty burn on your forehead as it moved up and down. Although we children were told to keep away and stand clear, we could not keep away. As the men at the top of the stack threw the sheaves of corn into the drum ears first, the drum growled – it seemed to be another hungry beast. If a sheaf was dropped in without the band being first cut the old drum would bang and rattle in protest, the engine would give an almighty chaff, and sometimes the belt would be thrown off. This would annoy the driver, who by this time was nodding off, as the result of a combination of the warmth and the gentle rocking of the engine. The straw came out one end of the drum to be tipped on to the elevator which took it up to the stack where it was removed by two men. The stacker had to be very skilled. He had to build the sides of the stack straight while the middle had to be filled so all formed a free-standing pile, like a straw house. Very rarely were they lop-sided. The stacker had to remember how he built the stack so that when it had to be taken down, that could be done without a lot of trouble. The grain ran from the drum like a golden river into sacks. We would put our hand in and feel the hard grains rush down. Then corn was weighed in what was known as coombs. The weight of a coomb varied according to what the sack contained. A coomb of wheat weighed 18 st., a coomb of barley, beans or mustard seed weighed 16 st. These were carried on men's backs, often long distances to the barn or granary and often up very rickety stairs and across planks. As the sacks were filled they were sown up and stacked. It took strong hands and backs to move them.

Later on the farmer bought a sack winder. This was a machine with a platform that was cranked up with a rope and a ratchet. The sack was put on the platform and raised by turning the handle until it was high enough for a man to get it comfortably on his back. My job was to crank the sacks up. Releasing the ratchet dropped the platform with a lovely thud. Of course we children wound each other up and down when nobody was about – a practice strictly forbidden by my father, but he never knew. Then there was the chaff, this flew out from under the centre of the drum, it puffed and blew out into an incontrollable pile, which had to be put into sacks. It was all very dirty, dusty, noisy and dangerous, but we loved it. The chaff was bagged up and carted away for cattle and horse feed and was kept in the chaff house. We didn't play in there very often, because when we got home and took our clothes off there would be a lot of chaff on the floor and that didn't please mother one little bit.

A net was put round the stack, when we were threshing, to catch the rats. As the stack grew smaller the rats began to rush out, terriers caught most of them as they tried desperately to get away. Boys with sticks tried to get the remainder; we were paid a penny for each tail, and as money was scarce every little helped. During the war years it was compulsory to use a net and several farmers were fined heavily for not doing so. All the old hands in the threshing gang tied string round their trouser legs just below the knees to stop rats running up their trouser legs. It had been known and was very nasty.

Life was simple enough for us to be able to do most things for ourselves. Chimney sweeping had to be done once a year. My father did this helped by myself as I grew older. Twigs were tied together on a rope and pulled up and down the chimney. It removed the soot from the side of the chimney but put most of it on the kitchen floor. This happened even though a large piece of sacking was fixed over the mantelpiece. Sometimes my father was a bit reckless and set fire to the soot in the chimney. He would get a large bundle of dry straw, soak it in paraffin, push it up the chimney as far as he could reach and then set light to it. The sparks and smoke billowed out of the chimney in a large cloud. It was crude but very effective. Of course he had to ensure that the sparks and red hot soot blew away from the stackyard and the buildings.

Getting About

When my father could spare time off from his garden at weekends we occasionally went out for a bike ride. We took sandwiches and rode around the local villages.

There were no signposts, but my father knew his way around all the byways. We sat and had our picnic in a field or on a grassy bank. Then we played a while before we set off home again. When a child was too young to pedal his or her own bike my mother had a basket seat fitted over the back carrier and the child was strapped into this. Some women had a small seat strapped to the frame just behind the handle bars, this enabled her to take a toddler on the front seat and a smaller child on the back. A child carried like this would be wrapped up very well with leggings and scarves to keep out the cold, but sometimes our hands got very cold which led to 'cold aches'. When we got home we put our aching hands in cold water and dried them on the cat's fur but sometimes we cried with the pain. As we got older we had to learn to ride a bike, both my sister and myself learned at the age of three. Our first bike was a little solid-tyred machine, just two wheels, no stabilizers, and we fell off many times, but we learned to fall without any real hurt apart from a few grazed knees and elbows. The more you fell the quicker you learned.

A bike was the only means of transport. All the shopping was brought home in bags hung on the handle bars, bigger items could be balanced on top of the handle bars. It is surprising what could be brought home on a bike, with a little determination. There was very little traffic in those days, it would be too dangerous today.

Mothers coming home from market on Tuesdays and Saturdays with shopping would frequently have a toddler on the front seat, a small child strapped on the back seat and bags balanced on each side of the handle bars. The shopping had to be collected and this was the only way to get it home. The men seldom went shopping with their wives. When children had their own bikes parents would often give them a hand by pushing them along by the shoulder into a head wind, but we still had to pull our own weight. Bikes were as common in families as cars are today.

My father was a complete countryman, he could hedge and thatch, swing a scythe and cut hay in beautiful straight lines. Every so often he would get his rub-stone out from his belt and with quick easy strokes the scythe would be keen again, then back to a lovely swinging rhythm that took real skill. He knew what should be done to the crops and when to do it. He had a fair idea about how the weather would be by looking at the sky morning and night. Husbandry like that seems to have been lost as machinery and chemicals have taken over.

One job we did on winter evenings was make rugs for the hearth. We got the rag bag out, no rag was wasted, the rags were torn into strips about one inch wide by five inches long. A piece of sacking was collected from the barn and using a special hook the pieces of rag were pegged into the sacking in a patchwork pattern style. When the pattern was finished another piece of sacking was used to back this and it made a very useful and colourful hearth rug. But it took a strong arm to shake the dust out.

Mother

My mother had been a housemaid before she married. We loved to listen to her tales of life below stairs. In some houses it was very hard work with not very kind bosses. Her last position treated her as one of the family. As a child she was always getting in scrapes or getting lost. Never once did she not get up to get my father his breakfast before he went to work.

In the garden of the council house my mother had a patch of violets. When these were flowering she made neat little bundles with leaves round the flowers and tied with raffia – these were sent for sale. When we went to the cottage at Greenham a clump of these went with us and grew in the garden. My mother made a lot of our clothes, she always seemed to be knitting something. She used to do seasonal work too, strawberry picking, potato picking and helping at harvest time.

The garden of the council house was about a half acre. Some of this was set aside for strawberries, which we picked and sold, the wooden chips were paper lined, the fruit was paper covered and stacked by the roadside for collection. We went strawberry picking for a neighbour who had an acre or two of strawberries and the season lasted five or six weeks. It was hard labour but great fun. As we grew older and went to the senior school we had a fruiting holiday which lasted for three weeks.

Sickness

When anybody was sick it was a long trip to call the doctor for there was no phone. In those days, before the Health Service it was a strain on the family budget because the doctor had to be paid, and there was little left from the household expenses to pay him. So the doctor was called only when absolutely necessary. When my sister had the measles the house was fumigated on her recovery, the door and windows of her room were sealed up, her toys and books were piled up in the middle of the room, and a kind of 'smoke bomb' was lit. When one of the children was sick with an infectious disease the other children were not allowed to attend school. We were usually very healthy considering that we had to ride to school in all weathers and lived most of our lives outside. Perhaps it was due to the good wholesome food and fresh air and exercise.

Samphire

Another childhood delight was samphire picking. Samphire is a delicious seaweed that grows in the mud of the salt marshes, and the best samphire grows on beds that are washed by the tides twice a day. A samphire picking trip had to be planned with care, the marsh was a dangerous place for those who did not know it, or times of the tides. As the tide came rapidly in the creek filled with water, so we had to be sure we were back on the bank before that happened. We sometimes had wide creeks to jump. Father would jump first, the samphire bag was thrown over, then we children jumped towards his outstretched hand. Sometimes we got a bit wet. Once we got soaked.

We always went out over the marsh in our bare feet, the mud oozing deliciously between our toes. As the samphire is ready in July we were not cold. We took only the bushy plants that grew along the sides of the creeks. The samphire came out of the mud with a lovely sucking sound. When we had our bags full or the tide was beginning to creep up the creeks we made our way back. We washed the samphire in a deep pool of salt water, then put it in the trailer attached to father's bike. Then he went off to the village where it was quickly sold. Our bag was taken home where the roots were cut off and it was washed in clean water. It was put to boil till the fleshy part could be stripped from the woody skeleton. We ate it with vinegar and pepper, stripping it straight into our mouths. Some people eat it with butter but this is wrong.

First Employment

I left school at Easter 1944 and for six months I worked for a milkman. The milkman's father had his own cows and he bought milk from other farms. My first job in the morning was to go round on a tricycle and collect this in ten or twelve gallon churns. The only equipment we had was a cooler, a washing machine, a boiler and a separator. Deliveries took about four hours. I could see little future in this job so I left after six months. I wanted to learn a trade so I decided to become a blacksmith.

CHAPTER NINE

DERBYSHIRE DAYS

*Like many countrymen of his generation Mr Brian Frith is
very concerned about the changes that have occurred in
farming methods and he advocates a return to the more
natural organic methods that were practised in the pre-war
period. He starts with an account of his early experiences
and of life on the farm in his childhood.*

I was born on 7 May 1916 in the Nightingale Home at
Derby. At that time my father was away in the army
and my mother helped her parents on their small
holding. My first recollection was of the war ending
when I was two. I remember all the joy, singing and
shouting. I couldn't understand why my father couldn't
come straight home.

My first school was on the Ashbourne Road, Derby.
My aunt was the headmistress but I didn't benefit from
that, she was stricter with me than with anyone else. I
was always in trouble, always in fights. The school was
a horrible old building with miles of corridors. I didn't
like that school. When my father came home we were
able to get a bungalow on the estate of Lord Lonsdale.
My father worked in the estate management office. He
was a sort of trouble shooter, dealing with the legal side

regarding the tenant farmers. I enjoyed going with him on his rounds riding on the crossbar of his bicycle. I was made welcome by the farmers' wives who gave me a glass of milk or home-made lemonade, bread and cakes. When my father moved to Sponden to work on the Lechhole Park Estate I was sent to Sponden House School. Then I was sent to the Diocesan School in Derby because my aunt wanted me to become a priest, but that did not suit me and I returned to Sponden House School.

When I was fourteen I left school and soon found out that I learned more in the first year at work than I had in all my years at school.

I used to help my mother on washdays turning the dolly pegs and the wringer. I am glad to say things have improved now and women don't have to work so hard. My mother's hands were as rough as sandpaper with all the work she had to do. In those days women were beasts of burden.

When I was a child I had to go to church up to four times on a Sunday, this made me resentful and put me off religion for life, but I had an enjoyable childhood for there was always something to do in the countryside. We played marbles, conkers, hopscotch and football, and at school I was captain of the boxing team. When I left school I worked on my relatives' farms, then to get more money, I got a full time job with a farmer outside the family. I enjoyed this, you were like one of the family. The work was harder than today, but I enjoyed that work better than I did in the later part of my life when farming had become mechanized. In the early days farming involved a close relationship with the land and the animals.

I was recently watching a television programme in which a farmer held up two lumps of what looked like sloppy mortar in his hands and complained that his soil got so water-logged now that he was scared that if we had a hot summer his ground would turn into concrete. Of course it would – they had put so much artificial fertilizer on the land and no humus, and consequently the soil is starved of humus. If there was more humus in the land it would not get so soggy. Humus will soak up the water which will remain there. When the weather is hot and dry you have a reservoir of water in the soil – humus containing the moisture. They have forgotten how to keep the soil in a good condition. This happens particularly on arable farms where the land gets no animal manure. But animal manure is not what it was, for it is now sprayed on the land as slurry – it has the nutrients in but no humus. Straw is now burned but it was one of the most valuable things on the farm. It was used as bedding for animals in the winter and then used as manure. Manure was put into a midden and left to rot down for a year. You always used the previous year's supply of muck which had had time to rot down to a beautiful compost with good texture and not much smell. My grandfather used to say, 'There is nothing so honest as land but there is nothing so wicked as land if you are dishonest with it.' If you don't put in what you take out the land will suffer and so will you. Another old saying was 'If you look after the land it will look after you.' Farmers now take so much out of the land and put so little in. Artificial fertilizers are good for the crop, but after the crop is taken out nothing is left. If you use animal manure you still have the humus left.

The system of crop rotation we used worked like this. If you cropped wheat you didn't use sprays or fertilizers, insecticides or herbicides. After harvest the crop was stacked while you waited for the threshing machine, the straw would be gathered (not baled), carted and used for bedding. Quite a lot of herbage and spillage was left in the field. A good farmer would turn his sheep on the field to graze for a week or two and they would eat up the herbage before it seeded, that prevented weeds growing in the crop next year, but anyway you didn't put the same crop on that field next year. When the sheep had cleared it you would turn the Christmas chickens out and they would eat the spillage and get a lot of the insects out of the ground. When the land was clear you mucked it with last year's muck thrown on from a cart, though some farmers would take it on a tipper cart, dump it and then send a man to spread it. It was hard labour. When it was spread the birds would scratch it and eat the grubs, so there was no need to use insecticides or weed killers.

On washdays we never wasted the soapy water. It was always used to spray the vegetables. It washed the aphids off the plants but did not kill the useful insects. We were suspicious of insecticides for we thought that what killed insects might also kill us and other wildlife. By the use of insecticides we have killed off many wild birds, not only by killing the insects they would eat but also by poisoning the food that is left for them to eat.

At harvest time everyone worked hard and we had a lot of casual labour on the farm and I've seen as many as twenty men come in for the midday meal and sit down in the kitchen. We had a huge scrubbed-top table with forms on either side. The meal consisted of meat and potato pies, rabbit pies and even pigeon pies, good wholesome grub and easy for the farmer's wife to prepare because she was also generally at work stacking in the yard. Everyone worked from the youngest to the eldest at this busy time.

Religion was very important at harvest and Christmas. Even those who never went to church the rest of the year went at these times to say, 'Thank you Lord for the year we've lived and worked.' Religion is closely related to the land. If you believe that God created the earth, you are working on one of his greatest creations, but I've never been very religious.

During the war I was in the army. When I returned the land had been torn up by open-cast mining and I had to get a job in the pits. I got a small holding and worked on that during the day. Then the council compulsorily purchased the land, so I left and got a job on a farm in Leicestershire looking after the poultry on six hundred acres. But poultry farming is not the same now, the poultry are not treated as birds any more but as egg-laying machines or as something to kill and eat. They do not taste like chickens any more because they are killed at eight to ten weeks old before they are fully developed. Now they tell you to eat chicken to cut down the fat, but there is more fat in chicken than there is in pork. Now that we go for quantity not quality we have lost all sense of taste and of enjoyment in our food.

In the old days farmers' wives had stalls in the markets where you could buy real chickens, mainly young cockerels or perhaps old boilers, that were hens that had got too old to lay eggs – they needed more cooking than young chickens. On these stalls there were huge piles of eggs arranged by size and they varied between 1s. 6d., and 9d. a dozen. My mother and grandmother were very proud of their prize Rhode Island Red chickens. They were huge birds weighing eight to ten pounds each. The cockerel was a beautiful bird, very proud of himself, with a bronze coloured body, black wing tips and tail tips and a huge comb. People who kept Rhode Island Reds also kept Sussex chickens. If you put Sussex hens with Rhode Island cockerels you could sex the chicks as soon as they hatched. The pullets followed their father's colour and were bronze gold but the young cockerels were white silver like their mothers. The cross between these two breeds produced a buff coloured bird but their eggs were not so brown as those of the pure Rhode Island Reds. Since then careful breeding has produced a bird that will lay brown eggs.

The heavy breeds such as Rhode Island and Sussex were good layers but they were also good eaters. Each bird would eat about 8 oz. of food a day. They were very expensive to keep. Now the new hybrids can lay well on only 4 oz. a day. Today people are greedier, all they think about is the quantity of eggs they can produce. But thank goodness we are beginning to get back to organic production.

When I was a kid we had a huge joint of beef on Sundays which always had a beautiful ring of fat round it. From this mother got the dripping which we ate on our bread all week. Nowadays people have never heard of dripping. We ate vegetables straight from the garden, there were no freezers so you planned your garden so that one crop followed another and there was always some kind of vegetable in season. One of the few vegetables we preserved were runner beans. We used large preserving jars with screw-on tops. We put a layer of salt in the bottom of the jar and on this a layer of sliced beans, then another layer of salt until we reached the top when we finished with a layer of salt. The jar was sealed and kept in a cool place. They were brought out as a treat at Christmas. We poured the beans out washed them and left them to soak all night in water to get the salt out. We also bottled fruit in screw-topped jars and made jam. We used a lot of herbs too. When gathered they were hung in paper bags until they were dry and then they were put in jars. They were used to flavour the food.

Many old remedies were used. At weekends mother always gave us senna tea, she used to put raisins in to give it a better flavour. She also often gave us brimstone and treacle, and when we had colds we were given raspberry vinegar. Bread poultices were used on septic wounds or boils.

I can't remember an agricultural trade union in this district before the war, but I do remember the Jarrow marchers. The local people were horrified to see the condition of the marchers and the look of hopelessness on their faces. We tried to help them; trestle tables loaded with food were put out and we put them up for the night in barns and in the church. I'm afraid we are returning to those conditions again with this 'I'm all right' philosophy.

When I worked in the mines for seven years I joined the union, but when I went back to the farm there was no union around until one day a representative came round. Some of us then joined the union. Unionism was difficult to organize in agriculture for most farmers only employed two or three workers and the farms were a long way apart.

When I became a farm manager in Leicestershire there were twenty-seven workers on the farm most of whom belonged to the union. We had regular meetings of all workers and at these meetings we would discuss any grievances, which were always settled amicably. Strikes were never mentioned for they were too fond of the animals to leave them without food for a day.

It is different now that things have become mechanized. When I was a boy and I used to go round the farm with my grandfather we knew every animal by name. One thing that was very bad in those days was the slaughtering which was done on the farm before humane killers were used. In those days the pole-axe was used on cattle while pigs were hung up and their throats were cut. These methods were cruel and disgusting particularly when they were carried out by unskilled persons. Of course, the slaughter of poultry is still a cruel process.

There were many marvellous old country characters about in those days. One was the publican in our village. He owned the local bus which ran once an hour. It was an old Chevrolet twenty-two-seater, held together with wire and string. We children loved it, we would say, 'Go on Joe put your food down'. He was only five foot six tall but he weighed sixteen stones, not fat but muscle and he was a very powerful man. He had a small holding as well as the pub, and his wife had a riding stable. On Sunday he would put out cold beef, bread, butter and pickles on the counter of the pub and his customers could help themselves to as much as they liked. He had a brother Jack who would come into the bar looking like a tramp, though he had plenty of money; he carried a ferret in one pocket and some rats in the other. He would take bets that the rat could kill the ferret and it always did. He would also bet that he could worry a rat to death himself without getting bitten. When the bets were laid he would drop the rat out of the bag on to the counter and before it had time to move seize it by the back of its neck in his teeth and kill it. He could be objectionable at times but even when drunk could dodge any punch thrown at him.

We had our own well. There was a pump in the village and a few people in the centre of the village had tap water. Most people had dry pail lavatories and the night soil cart came round once a week to empty them. The night soil was emptied into a field, by this field there was a wood where there were many rabbits and sometimes a villager who had perhaps drunk too much would go out poaching miss his footing and fall into this stinking pit of manure. You knew who had been poaching the next morning!

Most people in the village were friendly and you never had to lock your doors. There were always dogs who would warn you if there were strangers, but the only time you got anything stolen was when townsfolk were about.

CHAPTER TEN

CHANGES ON THE FARM

*Many of my correspondents were saddened by the great
changes that had taken place in farming since the thirties.
As we have already seen in the contribution by Mr Frith
one of their main concerns has been the effect of the use of
chemicals on the land. While Mr Sheppard from Suffolk
shares that concern he also comments on the effect of
mechanization on the quality of life in the countryside.*

All the years I spent with horses and cattle I thoroughly
enjoyed, things were quiet and peaceful, listening and
watching the wildlife around us, walking up and down
the fields whistling and singing. You could talk to the
other horsemen when you were ploughing because we
had to work what was called four yard stretches. Within
two years [of starting work] I was in charge of three
colts pulling a double farrow plough. Peace and tran-
quillity filled the air. This went on for several years until
in came the tractor, but I must say, before I talk about
the tractor, the soil was mucked on a certain field in
rotation every year. The result was good healthy men

and women who never stopped away from work, not even when they caught a cold.

Farm workers were the lowest paid workers in the country which resulted in a very tight budget for every mother and father, but we worked on, and not because of money but our love for the land, the animals and the wildlife around us.

That is some of the good news, Now this, I regret to say is some of the bad news, which I think is disastrous not only for England but for most agricultural countries. Around 1935 we had one tractor delivered. It took-over nearly all of the ploughing on this 1,000-acre farm. Year by year more tractors were bought and in a matter of ten years we had fourteen tractors. The farmer bought land. Greed for more money came in, not for the worker but for the farmer. The horse, tumbril and wagon disappeared. I was riding about on a cold iron tractor seat.

Our ears were filled with the drone of an engine. We no longer heard the birds singing. The sound of the chains on the horses harness jingling and all nature's cries were gone forever. Trailers replaced wagons and mechanized farming took over.

But worse was to come. Farmyard manure disappeared and was replaced by fertilizers and the ground started to get poisoned. At first the fertilizers were sown and harrowed in, then the corn was drilled. That wasn't quick enough so they brought in a combined drill which sowed artificial fertilizer and corn together, the fine granules consisting of nearly 50 per cent nitrogen. Then problems arose, if the drill was left two or three weeks before it was properly cleaned out the whole drill seized up, so that the manure box part of the drill had to be replaced by new parts and that was expensive. It made me think, if that stuff rusted iron, what was it doing to the human stomach? They scrapped that idea and introduced separate manure and seed drills.

Next they brought in chemical sprayers which replaced the horse hoes. Weeds were sprayed instead of being hoed and left to die. Slowly but surely the earth was getting saturated with chemicals. When spraying I used to think, 'Some of this must be getting down to the water table'. When I came home after spraying all day my wife said my clothes reeked with chemicals. That meant a change of clothes and a bath. The cans containing the stuff we sprayed on sugar beet had the word 'Poison' on them and instructions to bury the empty cans.

Mr Sheppard went on to discuss his early experiences in more detail.

When I was working with horses, it involved getting up and getting to work at five o'clock in the morning to bate the horses so they were ready to work at seven o'clock. Our day was from seven until five o'clock at night including Saturdays and on Sundays we had to come in for nothing to feed the horses. No holidays only Christmas Day and if that fell on a Sunday you got no holiday at all. My first week's wages were 10s. 10d. I gave my mother the ten shillings for my keep, for food and clothes. It was a struggle to live. Next year I got a rise to £1 10s. Several years passed then in came the tractor. The wooden pole for the horses was replaced by a draw bar. I quickly learned to drive the tractor, it was a good thing really as those poor horses used to sweat so much their backs and shoulders turned into a white lather.

When the tractors and machinery took over the farmer gradually started to sack the men because they were no longer needed. Throughout my working life I lived in a tied cottage so if you didn't work on the farm you were slung out of your house, furniture and all. When I got married in 1949 I had to look for a job on a farm with a house as I was still living with my parents. I was lucky, I found a job in the neighbourhood on a farm run by two brothers. I worked for them for only one year. One brother died, the other carried on a little longer then tragedy struck again; we had foot and mouth disease. The pigs and cows were slaughtered. It was complete chaos, I did not sleep much for a whole week. It was a nightmare for me I couldn't bear the thought of them being killed, I had to drag them to a big hole to be buried.

From then my life was directed to machinery. I developed a mechanical mind full of the drone of engines and equipment, but I would prefer the peace and quiet of the age of the horse.

CHAPTER ELEVEN

A LINCOLNSHIRE LIFE

Sent by Mr G. Cottingham.

I was born in the month of November in the year 1912. My birthplace was a farm cottage in the parish of Fishtoft near Boston in Lincolnshire. This particular area has a notable link with the past. It was from a place here, called Scotia Creek, that the Pilgrim Fathers took ship for Bristol en route for America. There now stands a memorial on that spot to commemorate that occasion.

My father was employed on the farm there and my family consisted of him, my mother, three sisters and myself. I also had a brother but he was born some twelve years later so didn't figure in our earlier history.

My father always wore trousers of the Victorian or Edwardian era and would never wear the new-fashioned fly-fronted type. He wore a blue pair of corduroys for leisure and brown corduroys for work, the latter had a distinctive and not too pleasant smell when new but this soon wore off. They were gathered just below the knee by a pair of short leather straps often called 'yorks' or 'lallygags'. While working he wore a spotted neckerchief, this was crossed under his braces and tied on a bow at the front, this gave a slightly

Tyrolean effect. His boots for work were of strong fairly supple leather and heavily nailed which he kept well cleaned and dubbined with a leather preservative, each week. He never had any shoes and his Sunday boots had a number of hooks and eyelets to be fastened with.

His schooldays were of brief duration, he left at twelve. He paid 1d. per week for his education and, in spite of the brevity of his schooling, he was a good scholar. His ambition was to be a policeman but he was not tall enough for this.

One of his valued possessions was his cycle. It was a little out of the ordinary in that the wheels had their rims turned inwards and were referred to as beaded rims. This meant that the tyres had to be beaded-edged too as the modern wire trimmed type would not fit. When mounting the machine he would put one foot on the step, fixed on the back axle, and with a few vigorous hops would gain the saddle. There was only one brake fitted, this was on the front wheel so a too sudden application of this brake could mean that the bike and rider parted company.

My mother also had to pay 1d. for her schooling and was a good scholar too for that era. Before her marriage she delivered the local mail; this entailed crossing the River Witham by ferryboat as the iron bridge was not constructed until the year 1900. For a large part of her life she wore boots that buttoned at the side and were really quite smart. She told us children that the skirt of her wedding dress had seven yards of material in it, this was quite usual for the Edwardian period. She had a bike also. This was a Sunbeam fixed-gear model with a 28 in. wheel at the front and a 26 in. wheel at the back. I learned to ride this machine and quickly found that, unless you were pretty smart, the bike and rider soon parted.

To entertain us on the winter evenings my mother played the harmonium and we gathered round to sing songs and hymns. We also used to make snip rugs to put down on the floor. Some people used to make these rugs and then sell them.

The cottage where we lived was typical of its kind. There was, chiefly, a scullery, kitchen, sometimes a parlour or sitting room and a pantry with a raised brick shelf for salting a pig on. The upstairs accommodation comprised either two or three bedrooms. The scullery had a large copper in one corner. This was heated by a coal fire underneath it. The first task on a Monday morning was to get the fire lit and some water heated for the weekly wash. The other items needed on washday were a wash tub, a mangle and a dolly-tub complete with doll pegs. It was almost a day-long task as many of the clothes had to be starched and some rinsed in blued water, this treatment made them whiter. The kitchen was fitted with a cast-iron range. The oven sat on one side of the fire and the boiler for heating the water on the other. There were a few different types of ranges but the principle was the same. My father prepared his fire-lighting material each weekend. He made up a bundle of different sizes of sticks for each day of the week. Arising between 5.30 and 6.00 a.m., he would clear out the ashes from the previous day, put some paper in the bottom of the grate, then lay the sticks, small ones at the bottom and the larger pieces at the top. Next he placed the filled kettle on the top of the sticks and put pieces of coal around the kettle and lit the paper. By this time the kettle was boiling and the coal burning but all the sticks had gone, when the kettle was removed the fire was going well and the breakfast was ready. Some women hung a short metal shelf on the bars of the grate, this enabled them to put a flat iron near the fire. When the iron was hot enough, tested by dabbing a wet finger on the iron, another iron was put to the heat and in this way the ironing was done. My mother used to put her irons in the hot oven, she said the face of the iron kept much smoother this way.

When we went to town on a Saturday, we went in the carrier's cart. This was a horse-drawn vehicle and was owned by one of the villagers. This was a great treat for us, particularly at the annual May Fair, when we came home laden with brandy snaps, Grantham gingerbread and lots of other goodies.

The ordinary Saturday nights could be quite entertaining. If we had any money we could buy enough fruit to supply us for the week with a shilling, sweets and chocolate too went cheaply. One kindly event stays in my memory. Each Saturday night, after nine o'clock, one of the town's butchers would open up the back door of his premises and give away joints of meat to anyone presenting themselves there. Many poor people were thus able to enjoy the type of Sunday dinner that would have otherwise been denied them.

We children attended the village school and the Sunday school, and sometimes went with our parents to evening service. I can also remember celebrating the end of the First World War. This was a cause for much happiness and distribution of goodies.

Pre–1920

In those early days, the wages for single men were fixed at the hiring fair. This was on 14 May and was known as 'Pag Rag' day. Prior to this all men seeking re-employment would have packed all their possessions in a large tin trunk and have gone to their parents for a week's holiday. Come the 14th they would go to the fair and, after a certain amount of haggling, would agree on a certain sum. They would then adjourn to a nearby inn where the newly engaged men would be given a coin called a 'fastening' penny. Once this was taken a man was, in honour, bound to keep his bargain to his new master. When I was offered the coin I refused at first as I was reluctant to commit myself, but the offer of a 10s. note soon overcame my scruples. This being settled, I set off a few days later with my tin trunk packed. At the hiring fair some girls were hired as domestics by either the farmer's or the foremen's wives, but I am not sure whether they were given the 'fastening' penny. The man would be paid at the end of each year. Depending on his age and status on the farm he could get anything from twelve pounds down to five pounds [this wage appears to relate to a farm servant who lived in]. At this time of the year he paid all the debts accrued by that date, this consisted mainly of what was owed for clothing and footwear. The tailor would journey from farm to farm measuring his prospective customers. After this the articles were made and delivered and a settlement made at the end of the year. As far as I know no one defaulted. Sometimes during the year a man would draw or 'sub' a little of his money for luxuries from time to time. The more careful men kept as much cash intact as they could.

1920–30

The farm where my father worked changed ownership, so when 6 April came we moved. This day was always the day for country people to move house. Some of the more restless souls moved each year, others maybe quarrelled with their boss, in which the clincher was 'I shall want your house come April'. The moving process was done by the new employer by sending two horses and a wagon. All the bits and pieces were loaded on to the wagon along with the family and off they went. Very few of the families had an excess of worldly goods, so one wagon sufficed.

We children had to change our school and we now started to attend one of the town's council schools. It was an excellent school and we all of us made out quite well. Being a town school, country children were looked down upon by the town pupils, but all of us were resilient to this and it cut no ice. There were scholarships to be had for the Grammar School, but even if we had taken them and been successful, our parents would have been unable to maintain us there so we never tried to get there.

In the home we relied on paraffin oil for our lighting. The old duplex burner type of lamp was replaced by the new incandescent mantle. This gave a whiter, brighter light and we were delighted by the improvement. We still relied on candles in the winter to light our way to bed. There was no mains water, so our supply came from either a well, fed by a spring or by percolation through the soil. The other system was storing rain water caught on the roof of the house by guttering, which flowed into a concrete-lined cistern which had to be cleaned out each summer when the level was low. Every cottage had an earth privy, mostly at the bottom of the garden. This too was cleaned out annually.

There was no Agricultural Wages Board then but a rate was generally agreed upon and was often supplemented by the man having a fat pig as part of his wages. This generally attained a weight of around thirty stones. Should the animal be above this weight then a cash adjustment was made.

In the case of the foreman he was allowed more than one pig. He usually had single men lodging in his house. They were looked after by the foreman's wife, sometimes with the aid of a young girl who had just left school. The foreman was also allowed a milk cow and his wife made butter, often selling it on the market along with any spare eggs from the poultry also allowed. These perks often added up to a reasonable income but a lot of work, particularly if many lodgers were kept.

The tradesmen were mostly mechanized by now and we had a butcher, a baker and a grocer calling each week. At Christmas each tradesman gave us a present. The butcher gave a pork pie, the baker a plum loaf and the grocer a packet of tea, all of which were most welcome. We obtained our milk, butter and eggs from a neighbouring farmer's wife for whom I bought the weekly papers as I came home from school. The kindly old shopkeeper gave me a bar of toffee for this service. These farming people were the owners of the first car I ever rode in. It was a large Humber open tourer and their son had a bull-nosed Morris with a dicky seat at the back. In the summer they used to graze their dairy herd by the roadsides and I used to help mind them. They also had a billy goat with the herd, which was believed by some to keep illness from attacking the cows.

In the late summer when the harvest fields were cleared, we used to drive the pigs down to the fields and they fed on any corn left behind. This was mostly the bean crop. Sometimes the pigs were awkward and would stray in which case they would have to be brought back with all possible speed, not an easy task as pigs are very cantankerous at times. The farmer also moved chicken huts on to the field to make sure nothing was left. Some gleaning was also done by women and children, but this was fairly rare with us.

Our postman was rather a character. He supplemented his income by hairdressing and taxidermy, and each Good Friday he brought round and sold to us hot cross buns.

The by-roads were only cart tracks with grass down the centre. When they became rutted they were filled in by barrowing granite from a number of heaps placed at intervals by the roadside.

The outstanding event of this period was the General Strike in 1926. This had far-reaching effects and seemed to accelerate the number of unemployed people. Nothing was quite the same afterwards.

This was the year in which I left school. At this time

children had to stay at school until they reached the age of fourteen, and with my birthday being in the middle of November, I left at the end of the Christmas term. There was very little work to be had so I started work as a farm boy in the following spring. The first job was to riddle potatoes, then leading the fore-horses in the corn drill and, with a staff, lead the horse in the horse hoe. In the autumn I was taught to plough with a two-horse team.

In this area of Lincolnshire we guided our team with a single rein or line as we called it. This is how it worked. The line was spliced on to a special leather rein, which has a length of chain fitted with a spring hook. The chain and hook were threaded through the near-side bit-ring, then behind the horse's jaw. The spring hook was then fastened to the far side bit-ring. A very gentle touch was needed when driving the horse. If you wanted the horse to come to the left then a gentle pull and a call of 'come here' would do the trick. If a move to the right was required a very light jerking movement and a cry of 'gee a bit' was all that was needed. This line horse would then move his companion in the required direction.

It was essential that all the team keep abreast of each other. This was done by attaching a leather rein, again with a chain and spring hook, from the neck rein (known as a bearing rein) and then clipping it on to the line horse's traces. If this horse should try to get ahead of his line horse this check rein would keep him in position. This worked very well. This horse would also have a halter or piece of rope attached to his bit-ring and fastened to the line horse's collar. This acted as an aid for the driven horse to guide his mate by. If a two-horse team was being used, the line horse was always on the near side but a three horse team meant that he must be in the middle. Not all horses could be driven in this way and to get a really good line horse meant a lot of patient teaching when breaking in, but it was a great asset as only one hand was required for driving, the other could be used for guiding what ever implement was being used. Horses would only work in the position to which they were accustomed. If a horse was used to working on the left side of the team he would always have to be put there. No horse would work if he wasn't in his right position. Some wouldn't go between the shafts of a cart as they would kick and go to extremes if they didn't like this kind of work.

Winter ploughing was considered to be a very good job. The requirement for a day's work was about an acre for a single furrow plough and not quite two acres for a double furrow plough. There was another method of working a team. This was called 'bodkin ploughing'. For this a single horse was yoked in front of two. This horse was usually led by a lad and was used in very heavy conditions so that only one horse was working on unploughed land leaving one set of footprints. A skilled ploughman could set his plough so that once started from the end of the field he could put his hands in his pockets until he reached the other end, then he would just guide them round the headland and set them in position, then go with hands in pockets once more. There was always competition to see who could do it the best and the men would sometimes ride round to other farms and compare the drilling and ploughing.

Quite a bit of criticism was levelled at the not-so-good efforts and also if one farm's horses were not so smart as another. We mostly started the day with the exhortation, 'Now lads, here we go for a long day and a fine 'un' and most ploughmen would be whistling and singing all the time.

Our time in the fields was from 6.30 a.m. in the summer time, and 7 a.m. in the winter, until 2.30 p.m. When we brought the horses from work we fed them and then went in for our own dinner. We then came back and fed, watered and groomed the horses then went off for tea about 5 p.m. After this we gave them their supper and bedded them down finishing about 7 p.m. As we had been working, apart from mealtimes, since about 5 a.m. we didn't usually go out. Sometimes in the afternoon we had to cut the feed for the horses but steam-driven chaff boxes were often used. We also took any horses needing shoes to the local blacksmith.

On the potato growing farms the early crop was lifted and packed into barrels, then a covering of potato haulm was placed on the top and secured by short ropes fixed on the barrel. This prevented bruising of the crop and made them more presentable for marketing. The potato pickers were mostly the wives of the farm men. Quite a lot of the older ones wore a poke bonnet and a long skirt over which they wore a long apron often made of hessian, or 'hardin' as they called it. This apron was secured at the waist by tapes and lower down, below knee level, there were also tapes to prevent the apron falling forward as they stooped to pick the crop.

Two of the highlights of our working life were, firstly, the County Agricultural Show which was held in the summer over three days. The third day was favourite with most working people as a cheaper admission was charged. The venue for this show was changed each year in those days but it is held on a permanent site now. The second attraction was the annual ploughing match. This too had to have a fresh site each year. There were classes for land drainage and hedge layering. Most of the matches comprised horse-drawn ploughs, the tractor was not employed enough to warrant a class of its own. Nowadays these contests are organized by Young Farmers clubs and are wholly mechanized.

There were now a number of motor cycles about. The early ones had no kick-start so in inexperienced hands the owner of one of these would have to do a lot of running. The buses or charabancs were becoming commonplace. Some of these were open-topped but we were a hardy lot in those days.

The farm men often wore breeches and leggings when dressed up. The leggings, along with the boots, were always highly polished. This type of dress was replaced by the wearing of very wide-legged trousers. Known as 'Oxford bags', these were so wide that when worn no footwear was visible. However the real mark of sartorial adornment was a blue serge suit, and a dazzling white shirt. The whole thing was topped by a trilby hat. This was the epitome of Sunday best wear.

The girls' dress had also changed very radically. Known as flappers they wore tight-fitting dresses or skirts just above the knee, silk stockings, high-heeled shoes and a close fitting hat on short bobbed hair. Like the men, their pay was rather frugal. Domestics received about 10s. per week but their food and lodging was provided, whereas many who worked as shop assistants only received the same amount of money and still had to pay for their keep. They also had to be smartly dressed in keeping with the job, whereas domestics would often be supplied with a uniform of dress, cap and apron.

Towards the end of the twenties we saw the introduction of talking pictures, which were a great improvement on the silent films. I first saw a sound picture in 1930 and was very impressed. There were getting to be a few radio sets in the homes of the people. They were powered by a wet battery or accumulator which had to be charged once a week and was done by a neighbouring garage or a radio dealer. The early sets had no valves and were known as crystal sets. The programmes were broadcast by two radio stations, 2LO and 5GB. I believe one was from London and the other from Daventry. This added a new dimension to the lives of country people and made them more a part of the community. The radios rapidly improved and the old crystal sets soon gave way to sets with valves and loud speakers. This meant that everyone could hear the broadcasts instead of just the one wearing the headphones.

Our family didn't aspire to this luxury as the price of a radio was well beyond our means. Our source of evening entertainment was when my mother played the harmonium and we gathered around and sang. Our parents often sang the old music-hall songs of their era, some of which I have never heard elsewhere. Many homes had gramophones. These were rapidly improving in appearance and tonal quality. The old trumpet horn type was replaced by the new hornless type and were often built, along with a radio, into a beautiful cabinet thus creating a desirable piece of furniture. There were also some types of portable gramophone.

The wages were now fixed nationally and in Lincolnshire there was a two-tier system of pay. In the Holland division the wages were 3s. above the Lindsey and Kesteven areas. Thus in Holland the pay was 33s. which I believe was one of the highest in the country. There was an extra few shillings for horsemen, shepherds and stockmen which operated in all areas. There was a deduction of 3s. per week for rent and 9d. for National Insurance. I think overtime pay was 10½d. per hour, but very little overtime was worked.

Several of the larger villages had their own horticultural show and most of the lesser ones had garden fêtes and fairs. One of the main attractions was bowling and playing skittles for a young pig or a copper kettle. These competitions were usually dominated by experts who went from show to show. They would bowl until they had scored a maximum, then they would leave knowing the prize was theirs.

Most of the villages would occasionally have an evening whist drive and dance. The prizes were mostly given and all proceeds went to football clubs or national institutions. The local inn had its darts and dominoes teams also.

There were quite a few charities left by local benefactors. These took the form of coal, bread, some clothes and places at the Grammar School for local boys.

On the farms there was a big acreage of sugar beet being grown. This meant quite a bit more of seasonal work was available, but the Depression was very severe and times were quite hard.

In the early days, one of the main tasks was to clean out the crewyard and cart the manure into a big heap in a field where the manure was intended for use when the field had been cleared of its crop. The procedure was for two or three men to fill a cart in the crewyard; when full it would be replaced by an empty one. Then a driver would take it to the field for emptying. He would then take another one to the crewyard for refilling. Often the fillers would be on piece work and the average price would be 7s. per twenty cartloads. Another way was to measure the area of the crewyard, then the depth of the manure was measured and reckoned in cubic yards. After much haggling a price would be agreed upon and the work commenced. In the case of pricing by the cartload much argument ensued about the amount loaded on to each cart. The loads would be in the foreman's estimation too small but the job generally finished without too much acrimony.

The fields often seemed to shrink from the time of sowing to the harvest when two men stooked the corn. The first harvesting task was for two men to go to the field, one with a scythe and the other with a gathering rake. The man with the scythe mowed a swathe right round the field sufficiently wide enough to enable the two horses and the binder to go round the field without treading on the corn. The other man gathered the mown corn into sheaves. Then making a band of the same material, the sheaf was dropped on to it and secured by twisting the ends together and tucked into the band. When the sheaf was made it was stood tight to the hedge or otherwise out of the way of the coming binder.

In this farming era the corners of the field that were inaccessible to the plough would be dug by a man with a spade, who would then scatter some corn over it from a sack he carried with him. Another wintertime job was for a man to take a spade and throw onto the headland the seam of soil nearest to the hedge. This enabled any rubbish to be shaken out with the spring cultivations and was looked on as a mark of good farming.

A very useful conveyance often used for carting during harvesting operations was the hermaphrodite or 'mophry' as it was known. This consisted of a framework with a platform fixed on top and mounted on two wheels. It was joined to the cart by a Y-shaped piece of timber. Then the cartshafts, having been previously removed, were lifted on to this extension. This gave the vehicle as much capacity as a wagon but it was less likely to tip sideways, as the wagon had a very limited lock for turning. After harvest the 'mophry' was taken off the cart and stored away for the winter.

1930–40

In the early 1930s the electricity grid system came into being and the countryside became dotted with thousands of pylons carrying the current. These pylons ranged in size, from the huge steel erections to the small wooden ones used for local distribution. This was a great advance as before then electricity had been just for the towns. Now it gave its benefits to all but the most isolated places where it would have been uneconomic. In some places, the power would be supplied by owners of a generating set, these were mostly driven by diesel engines but a few were wind-powered. In many areas also the water was being piped to the country population. Many of the villages had a large supply tank erected and water was pumped into them by engines. These tanks were built high enough to maintain a good pressure of water and was drawn from standpipes in the village, or by the roadside, as an indoor supply of water was the exception rather than the rule.

The people of this era were of a mostly happy disposition. They appreciated each new acquisition as it came to them, and mostly sang, whistled and shared any new joke they heard. Even the people unemployed were seldom miserable. Everyone, workers and unemployed, were very hard up but we all did the best we could with our limited means.

In some areas we could augment our income by doing other jobs after our daily work was done. These jobs were natural and seasonal in the summertime. One of these was pulling peas for the early market. This was done by pulling the haulms from the ground, stripping the pods from the vines and dropping them into a basket. When full the basket was tipped into a small sack and when the sack was full of pods they were taken to the weighing maching and weighed. Each sack was entered against the puller's name and when work finished, or you had had enough, you were paid. Many of the people engaged in picking early potatoes in the daytime were women and girls. As their pay was only

3s. 6d. they could often double this in one good evening's work, and it had its social side.

There was by now a large increase in the number of motorized vehicles and consequently an improvement in road surfaces. On the farms the use of tractors was becoming widespread. The crawler tractor was in use for ploughing but the majority of tractors were iron-wheeled.

The Recession, with its high unemployment, still abounded. For many people unable to get dole their main source of income was parish relief. This took the form of vouchers for food and a few shillings in cash. To collect this relief we went once a week to a given place and received our dues from the local relieving officer. This gentleman was also registrar for births, marriages and deaths in the surrounding villages.

In the early thirties my father died and, as I was living at home, I had to help look after my mother and younger brother. We had to move house and went to a small cottage near Boston. Work was very difficult to obtain. Some of the farmers employed their men for three days a week, others employed half of the staff for one week, laid off the next, and then the other half of the staff worked. All in all they were very little better off than us on relief. Being on relief had a slight stigma attached to it. At the County Show men were given an award for long service but only if they had never been on parish relief.

The men on the parish, as it was known, were put to work digging out the huge drains that criss-crossed the fens and since there was no extra money forthcoming we enjoyed each other's company, since it broke the monotony of being idle and we didn't really work too hard. The use of mechanical excavators soon came into being and rapidly spread over the whole drainage area.

I did get a part-time job working on a fruit farm but it was only 'catch work'. After a time a family friend, foreman on a large farm, offered me regular work so this meant going into lodgings once more. I went home at weekends helping my mother as much as I could financially as her income was only 10s. per week and my young brother was still at school. I now entered a period of comparative affluence as we were often employed on piece work and we could mostly make an extra pound per week above the normal rate. For this we worked very hard indeed. When the potato crop was grown we had to hoe between each plant to loosen the soil and remove any weeds, for this we were paid so much per acre. In the autumn when the crop was lifted they were put into long clamps and given a good covering of straw, we then covered the clamp with its first coating of soil then following this coating of 4 in. was another 8 in. of soil, making a total of 12 in. altogether. The final touch was a capping of dyke mowings, or rodings as we called them. If these were not at hand, long straw would be used. The ultimate touch was to put spits of soil on this capping. It was very seldom that the potatoes came to any harm. If they were left in the clamp until late spring or early summer the sprouts would push through the coverings of soil so this covering would be removed.

When the market for potatoes was at a satisfactory price we processed them for selling. This was how it was done. While there were some mechanical sorters around at the time we did all ours by hand. Working in gangs of three we first of all removed, with spades, sufficient soil for what we thought would be a suitable tonnage. The next very important step was to construct a suitable windbreak so we could keep reasonably warm. This consisted of a number of long poles set into the ground and a large hessian stack sheet tied to these poles. The whole construction was then secured by guy ropes to keep it upright. The next step was to remove the straw covering from the potatoes, position the tools of our trade and prepare for action. The man using the riddle shook them around, picked off the unmarketable ones and then, with a neat motion of his arms, threw them into a sack positioned on a weighing machine. When the filled sack tipped the scales the third man removed it and quickly replaced it with an empty sack. He then either secured or tied the mouth of the sack. This whole process was repeated until after filling twenty sacks (one ton) we changed jobs. This went on all day and it took us twenty minutes to process a ton. For this the pay was 3s. so we needed quite a tonnage to make a bit of money. To make the job more interesting we competed with each other to see who could spill the least potatoes out of each ton. The winner was given a cigarette for his skill. For this price of 3s. per ton we had to grade the potatoes for seed and cattle feed and, when the lorry came to take them away, we had to load it up often carrying them on a broad plank spanning a wide ditch. At the time we were all young men and we could load a five-ton lorry in less than half an hour.

We also grew a lot of peas for the dried pea market and these were harvested by hand. Using a long-handled hook we cut them off at ground level and laid them in a row or in heaps behind us. On some farms they were packed on tripods and left out to dry. Whichever way was used they had to be left sufficiently long enough to be bone dry. When this stage was reached they were gathered and put into large ricks or stacks as we termed them. The stack was left to settle into shape and the roof was given a covering of thatch. They stayed there until the threshing machine arrived.

On our farm we had our own threshing tackle but a tractor was hired to drive it. Much of the threshed straw was baled and carted away. The corn was put into either twelve, sixteen, eighteen or nineteen stone sacks and, while it appeared to be hard work, once the knack of carrying these sacks was mastered it wasn't a bad job. Also an added attraction was the one extra shilling per day that went with the job.

In the spring of 1939 I moved once more. This time it was to a large sporting and agricultural estate. There were quite a few tractors, two lorries and some horses. The estate was owned by a titled family and had at one time been a priory converted into a beautiful family home. Heavy death duties necessitated selling the property so the priory was demolished, many of its contents being shipped abroad. The estate was made up of many types of soil from sand to heavy clay and was highly productive. I was now proficient in the more specialized jobs and could build and thatch ricks and layer hedges. These jobs I enjoyed doing but the more mundane tasks did not take my fancy. On all the farms where I had worked, with the exception of one, we had only one half hour lunch break which I enjoyed most when I was near a wood or river. I took delight in seeing the life of the woodlands or the riverbanks and my highlights were seeing the kingfisher and the otter. There were thousands of rabbits abounding and in my first season there were eleven thousand caught and sold.

In the late summer the Second World War began and everyone was exhorted to grow more food. The War Agricultural Executive came into being. They possessed a great number of tractors and other machines which were hired out to farmers. They also supervised a lot of farming operations telling the farmers which fields to plough up and generally keeping an eye on them.

After two years at this job I got married and as my wife had been her father's housekeeper previous to our marriage we stayed with him until a younger sister was old enough to cope with the job. My father-in-law was a farmer and my wife helped out on the farm work. They kept a few cows and my wife did the milking by hand. She also put the milk through the separator and once a week made butter from resultant cream. One of the by-products of the butter was residue left in the churn, known as buttermilk, this was the main constituent in cake making. Since my wife was an excellent cook many delicious cakes were enjoyed.

One of the products of the war emergency was the Women's Land Army. These girls were from all localities and all walks of life. On the adjacent farm where I was now working a number of these girls were employed. By and large they adapted themselves to the country way of life, some of them marrying and settling into the community. During the war years they were billeted in hostels or on the farms.

With the call for more land for cultivation the steam ploughing tackle was brought into use once again. They were not as plentiful as they had been in the 1920s but they did do a lot of work on our estate. Most of this virgin land was cropped with potatoes followed by cereals and being in very good heart the resultant crops were very satisfactory.

After living with my wife's family for a year we left and a house being available we moved back to my old employer's and I was now a tractor driver. The cropping was more varied now and a new crop for us was rye. This was practically unknown to us but the resulting straw, being very long and tough, made excellent material for thatching.

The war years brought back into use the old custom of keeping a pig for home consumption. A hut or a sty was provided in which the pig was housed and we were allowed coupons that permitted us to buy pig food. We took these coupons to our local miller for our supply of feed. The miller used water power to grind the corn and in the event of a water shortage he used an ancient tractor to see himself through. He also wove baskets as a sideline. Some tractors were now fitted with cabs to give the driver protection from the weather but it still remained a very cold job.

As time progressed we started a new venture. We started to grow green peas for the canning industry. They were harvested by manual labour then brought to a vining machine, packed into boxes and taken to the canning factory some miles away. This was the forerunner of the pea and vining industry but our produce was canned whereas now it is frozen.

There was also a new machine available for cutting the pea crop for the dried pea market. Using a three-wheeled tractor there was mounted in front of each wheel a metal torpedo-shaped shield. This guided the peas into swathes and these were cut at or just below ground level by three pairs of v-shaped knives mounted on a frame at the rear of the tractor. This was a much quicker and easier method than when it was done manually. Practically all wheeled tractors were fitted with new pneumatic tyres, adding greatly to the driver's comfort.

The winter and early spring of 1947 was very severe and cultivations were delayed until April. Following this we had a really hot summer. About this time we had our first experience of crop spraying. The early use of crop sprayers was confined to killing weeds in the cereal crops but soon many different types of sprays for different crops followed.

This year also saw the advent of our first combine harvester. It was delivered to one of the farms in a large crate and the fitters came and assembled it on the spot. It was quite a big machine having a cutter bar width of twelve feet. This was raised and lowered manually with the aid of a spring-assisted wheel and the cut corn was carried to the elevator by three canvases fitted with wooden laths. There was one canvas fitted each side of a flat deck and one in the centre carrying the corn to the feed elevator. The corn was pushed on the platform or deck by a sail consisting of flat pieces of wood on a spindle and driven by a power unit. This sail was replaced by a spring-lined pick-up reel made of metal. This invention was invaluable for picking up the lodged or laid corn, should the season be wet. The power unit was a six-cylinder Chrysler petrol engine and the fuel consumption was two gallons per hour. These early combines were very slow moving and an average day's work was about ten acres. The grain was graded in a cylindrical drum and was in three categories which were; the best, second class for bird seed and the last was mainly weed seeds. In fact a combine was no more than a mobile drum. From this drum the corn ran down through a fine screen into hessian sacks and when each sack was filled the top was securely tied and it was then put into a chute. When the chute was full a small door at the bottom was released and the sacks slid onto the ground to be picked up later by a team of men with trailers. This was quite hard work as the sacks were of twelve or sixteen stones in weight. A lot of the corn was taken directly to the merchants as corn driers were not widely used on individual farms. The combine was fitted with a sunshade which gave us some protection.

The use of combines necessitated a different method of clearing up the straw left behind so the use of balers became widespread. This was quite labour intensive but a large area of baled straw could be cleared in a day. The bales were stacked into large stacks then the roof was covered over with thatch or dyke mowings.

My wife and I had two growing sons and while they were interested in farming I thought they should have more choice in choosing a career than I had had, so we encouraged them to make the most of their educational opportunities.

Another area in which a lot of hard work came our way was sowing fertilizers on the land. There were quite a lot of machines to do this but we did it all by hand for a few years. It was one of the most tiring and hardest jobs we ever had to do. To do this task we were equipped with a large metal hopper strapped in front of us and supported by a strong heavy leather strap over each shoulder. The method was to fill the hopper with fertilizer. The capacity was between forty-two and fifty-six pounds in weight. Having filled up, the operator dipped his hands alternately and filling them with a practised motion spread the fertilizer on the ground. It was essential that while his hands were in motion the legs and feet should keep on even time otherwise the operator floundered all over the place. If the rhythm was lost the man would stop and start again. Depending on the needs of a particular crop we sowed any amount from two hundredweight to fifteen or twenty hundredweight per acre. The larger the amount the quicker the shovelling with the hands would have to be, but a small dressing meant taking a pinch between two fingers and a thumb and throwing it up and outwards. These small amounts required a good degree of accuracy because when sown on a growing crop the slightest bit missed showed up clearly and this brought on a lot of uncomplimentary criticism.

When sowing feritlizer for potatoes we had to walk down the rows ridged out for the planters. Sometimes the planters had to walk backwards and plant the potatoes singly which was a backache job. The chief essential for all broadcasting was getting the full sacks spaced out at correct intervals. Too close together meant having some fertilizer left when you reached the sack, too far apart meant there wasn't enough to reach the filling point.

The way we used to ensure accuracy in placing the sacks was done in this way. Having ascertained how much per acre the field was to receive we measured the area and, knowing the total acreage, we knew how many sacks would be needed; they would be placed onto the field in such a way that neither surplus nor shortage would occur. This measuring was invariably done by me while the other men loaded up the carts. Sometimes it was necessary for us to work overtime preparing the fertilizer for the next day's work.

We also sowed small seed such as grass, clover and mustard. Here precision was of the utmost importance. To ensure accuracy stakes were set into the ground to guide us from end to end. There was another method of sowing these small seeds. It could be done by a contraption known as a fiddle drill. It consisted of a small canvas sack fitted with a wooden chute, at the end of the chute a wooden bobbin was fixed. The other bit of equipment was a wooden bow fitted with a leather thong. This is what gave the outfit its name. As the seeds trickled down the chute from the bag the bobbin rotated by the action of the bow and the bobbin being fitted with metal vanes threw out the seed in a consistent stream provided a good rhythm was maintained.

In the summer months we did a lot of work among the sugar beet and the potatoes. This was done at piece work rates fixed by representatives of the Wages Board.

CHAPTER TWELVE

AN AGRICULTURAL
WORKER IN KENT

Mr L. Wallis, a true Kentish man, tells:

I was born on 4 July 1912 in a farm cottage at Chalk, Kent, the youngest of four sons. My birth was celebrated by my father with one of his friends singing to the accompaniment of a melodeon (accordion), seated in front of the cowshed opposite our cottage, I learned later that the melodeon was the only form of entertainment we had in those days.

At the rear of the cottage was a meadow where cows were put out to graze. In the front, as already mentioned, was the cowshed where the second eldest of my brothers, Bob, milked the cows twice each day, including Saturdays and Sundays. My eldest brother was ill after leaving school at fourteen and did not start work until he was twenty-one. My other brother was at school.

My father's job was to cart greenmeat (a mixture of tares, sainfoin and clover) which he cut with a scythe, to the local breweries in Gravesend, to feed the horses which drew the wagons delivering beer to the public houses. As I grew older I remember waiting for him to come home with the malt sugar used in the brewing of beer. This was very sweet and kept us fit and well.

I had one year at Chalk school when my father decided to move to another farm at Shorne; this was in 1918. All our furniture, clothes and possessions were loaded into a farm cart supplied by our new employer, and we set off to our new farm cottage in Shorne, approximately two and a half miles away.

The cottage was smaller than our previous one – two up and two down. Mum and dad had the front bedroom. We were a little cramped when we all left school. Mum did all the cooking on an iron kitchen range, the washing in a copper or in the stone sink. In this one room we had our meals and used it as a living room. You can imagine what it was like on washing day when the weather was wet, when mother was trying to dry the sheets and other things on a rope line tied above the mantelpiece. The front room, which today would be called the lounge was only used after tea on Sundays when we had visitors and at Christmas.

The loo was at the bottom of the garden, consisting of a wooden shed with a hole in a wooden seat and a metal bucket underneath, which my father or brothers had to empty at least four times a week. We had no bathroom so we had a weekly dip in a metal bath (in winter in front of the fire). At the back of our cottage was a brick building where, years before, the farm workers baked bread. Although it was almost intact with an oven, my father used it to store coal and garden tools.

We were a happy family and we often had a sing-song when my father played the mouth-organ. I think I was about ten when the family bought a gramophone, and some years later I built a crystal set. Then, of course, we had the wireless. I remember a great day in the village when we gathered at the village hall to hear King George V deliver the first Christmas speech on the wireless.

I attended Shorne Church of England School and had to walk at least a mile, mostly uphill, and in the winter through two feet of snow.

The farm where my father and brothers worked was run by two brothers, who lived in two houses about half a mile apart. When I was about twelve years old, my mother decided that I should earn some pocket money. My father got me a job at the farmhouse as a houseboy during weekends. The job consisted of cleaning the shoes, washing the stone floor of the dairy, exercising the gun dogs, cleaning the windows and so on. For this I received 1s. 6d. plus a cup of tea or cocoa, or a glass of milk and a piece of homemade cake.

Wages were very poor and I believe my father and brothers were paid 28s. basic per week, with overtime 32s. and a little more if they were a wagoner, looking after the horses. I also earned a few pence in the winter, scaring rooks off the freshly sown corn. Mother used to pack me a few sandwiches which I enjoyed in a hut or a shelter I had made from a few branches of trees, which supported the roof covered with sacks. This whole operation was known as 'bird minding'. I cannot think why, as we were in fact minding the corn. I carried a wooden rattle, similar to those carried by football supporters and a few turns would send the birds away. Some of my school friends would visit me during the day and if the weather was cold we would light a fire and bake potatoes. Another job I had was scaring birds from the cherry orchard. The farmer had rigged up a Heath Robinson contraption which made life a little easier. A rope was attached to a tree near the end of the orchard and slung over the branches of the trees to the middle of the orchard. Attached to this rope, at intervals of three or four feet, were pieces of tin sheet, tin cans filled with stones and anything that would create a noise. All I had to do was to tug on the rope at one end and, my God, what a din! I would then walk through the orchard and repeat the action at the other end of the rope.

During my school holidays, I was always happy in the hop fields. There was a hop field some 200 yd from our cottage and the work that was carried out preparing the plants was interesting for me. There was a giant tank at the end of the field, which we called a tar tank as in it the men heated a liquid and then loaded it with the hop poles, to prevent the poles from rotting. The poles were put into the ground at intervals where the hop plants were growing. When all the poles were secure in the ground a man on stilts tied yards and yards of string between the poles for the hop bines to cling to — something like the method we use for runner beans. When the hops were ready to pick, dozens of women and children from the towns came to pick them The children had great fun but were worn out at the end of the day. I used to make my way to the oast-house where our next door neighbour worked. His job was to dry the hops and then put them into pockets ready for transportation. He often allowed me to turn the handle of the press, and when the pocket was full it was weighed and the name of the farmer, its weight, etc. were stencilled on.

When I finally left school at fourteen years, I was employed full time at both farmhouses. I had to saw and chop wood, cut the lawns, feed the chickens and ducks, look after the ferrets, run errands to the men in the fields, help with the kitchen gardens. There was no water from the mains, so I had to pump the water from the well to a tank in the loft. I turned a big wheel, something like a mangle. But at the main farmhouse the pumping was done by a horse which was harnessed to a long arm while the horse was led round and round the pump house.

At the age of sixteen years I was paid 12s. 6d. per week and had to carry out normal farm worker's jobs (except looking after the horses). At harvest time, my father had to open the harvest fields ready for the horse-drawn self-binder. This meant that he had to cut with his scythe all round the field, a sufficient space to allow two horses to walk. He then had to tie into sheaves the corn he had cut. Then the self-binder cut down the corn over the rest of the field and after tying it up, deposited the sheaves on the ground. They were then gathered up by the other men and made into stooks or shocks. When all the sheaves had been collected up they were taken by cart to the stackyard where they were built in stacks that were thatched to keep out the wet weather. Later on in the year a threshing machine was hired by the farmer. This consisted of a steam-engine, thresher and a caravan in which the men operating the machine lived during their stay on the farm. The machine filled the sacks with corn automatically, but the straw fell loose on the ground and had to be baled by hand and tied using thongs made from the straw.

The sacks of corn, weighing 2½ cwt, were loaded into carts and transported to the granary. The only access to this was by a dozen wooden steps, and the men had to carry the heavy sacks to the huge wooden bins at the top. The granaries were built on stilts to prevent rats and mice getting at the corn.

Ploughing the fields to prepare for the crops was carried out by wagoners with one, two or four horses, depending on the type of plough used (in Kent the horsemen were called wagoners). The Run-Round was a single shear plough, requiring only one horse and it could be turned round at the headland without lifting the plough. The Balance was a single shear plough and on reaching the headland, it was tipped up ready to plough without turning the implement. It was drawn by two horses and if the ground was heavy, three were used. The Kent plough was a heavy, wooden instrument, drawn by four horses and had to be lifted off the ground to turn it round at the headland.

Potato planting was done by hand. The man or woman carried a box of potatoes, putting one potato at a time into the furrow. I have seen thirty men in a field carrying out this operation. Smaller seeds, such as beans, peas, cabbages, swedes and corn were either drilled or sown by hand. When the potatoes were ready to lift they were dug up by the men with the women picking them up and putting them into 1 cwt bags. All the greens were cut by hand. Before I left the farm, potatoes were being lifted by a horse-drawn spinner but the potatoes still had to be picked up by hand and put into bags.

It was a common sight to see twenty or thirty men hoeing the weeds. It must have taken days to finish the field. When the corn was some twelve inches high, the men and women were sent into the field to clear the corn of thistles, each person carried a long-handled tool called a 'thistle dodger'. This had a wooden handle with a small spade two inches wide at the end. This work was called 'thistle dodging'. When the peas were ready, crowds of women and children descended on the farms to pick the peas. The peas were put into sacks, weighed and transported by the men.

Before the days of the tractor, steam ploughs were hired by the farmers. Like the threshers, the operators had their own caravan to eat and sleep in during their stay on the farm. They had two steam-engines, each with a cable and drum fitted underneath the engine. The engines were positioned at each end of the field, a plough with six shears was attached to the cable and drawn from one end of the field to the other by the engine. Before I left the farm in 1930 tractors were slowly taking over from the horses but many years passed before the horses finally died out. Many of the tractors were very small and had metal tyres and spikes on the wheels, but they did not need crops to feed them.

Talking of feeding – my brother was a stockman for many years and not only did he feed the cattle and pigs but he also had to prepare their food under primitive conditions. There were hand-driven machines for chopping potatoes and wurzels, crushing oil cake and cutting straw into chaff. A wooden contraption called a 'riddle' was used for grading potatoes. They dropped through a grill that had various sized holes in it into three shutes where the large, medium and small (chats) were collected into sacks. The chats were boiled and mixed with meal and fed mainly to chickens and ducks. When the brussels and cabbages had been cut, the sheep were moved from the meadows on to the fields to clear the stalks and, of course, to manure the ground. There was not enough left of the greens to feed the sheep, so the shepherd brought them extra foodstuff in sacks. Some of this feed consisted of locust beans and when the shepherd was not looking we kids used to hunt through the sacks, for the locust beans contained sugar and were very nice to eat.

During the year a ploughing match was held on one of the farms. The wagoners spent days cleaning the horses' brasses, the harness and the plough, and of course, the day before they got the horse ready with plaited tail and mane. Depending on where the match was to be held, the wagoners would sometimes set off as early as 5 a.m. to get there in time. Gallons of beer were consumed on these occasions; and likewise at the annual market where farmers showed their best cattle, sheep and pigs.

All the produce, when collected from the fields, was sent to the local railway station by horse and cart to be loaded into railway trucks to be transported in this way, but the bulk of the harvest was stored in the granaries awaiting transportation by the buyers.

The farmers treated the farm workers well. Once a year a fête was arranged on the cricket ground, where all the farm hands together with their wives and children gathered for a real old-fashioned fun day. Usually at the end of the harvest the farmer laid on a charabanc to take the entire group of farm workers for a trip to the seaside. At Christmas the farmer supplied each worker with a joint of meat, so being a farm worker was not a bad lot considering the rent of his cottage was 2s. 6d. per week, plus perks like vegetables, eggs, cheap milk and the odd bird or rabbit when the farmer had his annual shoot. The vicar also supplied the poorer families with care at Christmas, helping to load and hump the coal himself. He also visited once a week on his bicycle.

There was always plenty to do after work. I went to evening classes at the village school, learned to dance at the Women's Institute social evenings in the village hall, acted in *A Midsummer Night's Dream* and played Sam Weller, in *The Pickwick Papers*. I played cricket for the local team, when the game was played in a friendly spirit.

The village I worked in and now write about has changed very little since those days. Of course there are many more houses and people in the main village, but the farms remain as they were in the thirties.

I married the parlour maid who worked at one of the farmhouses.

CHAPTER THIRTEEN

THE HIRING FAIR

Mr L.F. Maw of Selby, North Yorkshire, told us about the hirings that continued to play a vital part in the life of the farming community in the north of England in the 1930s, although they had ceased to function in many other parts of the country.

On 13 November each year we used to go to the boss as hired lads to receive our year's wages, and we had to tell him whether we were stopping for another year, or leaving. So, if you left, you used to go on the first Monday after 23 November and stand against the Old Cross in Selby, until some farmer or his representative came up to you and asked, 'Do you want hiring?' Then the argument would start.

Farmer: 'Dost ta want hiring lad?'

Lad: 'It depends on what tha's going to offer'.

Farmer: 'What is tha, a wagoner or a lad?'

Lad: 'I would like to be a wag' (as they called us who went with horses and wagons).

Farmer: 'I will give thee £26 for the year.'

Lad: 'I think I'll wait a bit to see if I am offered more.'

Farmer: 'I'll see thee a bit later.'

If we had not agreed with some other farmer by four

o'clock we would go to the first farmer who had offered £26 and say we would accept his offer. Then he would give us what they called a fastening penny, which amounted to 2s. 6d. He would then tell me where to meet him on the following Monday with my box of clothes and so on for my year's work ahead. We started work at six o'clock each morning and worked until six o'clock at night with one hour's break from twelve noon till one o'clock. We fed our horses before breakfast and again at night, then groomed them.

We hired lads lived with the foreman on the farm. If we got on well with him we were quids in, but if not, you were in for a rough year. The foreman I was with was fairly good, except for meal times, which were the same each day for every meal. We started off with boiled milk in a basin with a big lump of boiled fat bacon in it, for breakfast. Dinner was rabbit with vegetables, and rice pudding every day. Tea was boiled bacon and prunes. Supper, if we were in by ten o'clock, was apple pie with a pot of tea. But, if we were not in by ten o'clock, we were locked out and had to sleep in the stable, with the horses on the straw in the winter time. In the summer the horses were turned out in the grass fields.

In clover or hay time we got our horses groomed and harnessed up, ready for going out cutting with the reaper at 3 a.m. and worked until 1 p.m. Then we changed with the second lad who went on from one o'clock until dusk. Then the clover had to dry before it was raked up and put into the haycocks to dry some more. When it was properly dry it was collected up in wagons and stacked in the stackyard near the farm.

It was harvest time in August and September. After that, in October it was potato picking time. We had a gang of Irish men usually eight in number. We had to start ploughing the potatoes out about two hours before the men started picking them out of the rows. Two men used to pile them in long 6 ft wide heaps and then cover the heaps with straw on the sides, keeping it straight and then they put three layers of soil to hold the straw in place. Then when the frosts came the pie (as these heaps were called) was covered with more soil to keep the frost out.

In November we were ploughing the sugar beet out ready for the Irish men to chop the leaves off and put them into heaps. Then the farm labourers came and put them in carts and took them to the railway sidings where they were loaded into large railway trucks to be taken to the sugar beet factory in Selby. By then it was nearing 23 November, and we lads were looking forward to our year's pay.

It went on like this for two years or more. As I was the head wagoner on the four farms that our boss owned the lads started pushing me to ask the boss about overtime pay as we all thought it was time we should be paid for the long hours we worked after our usual time, in hay time and harvest. So I approached the boss with the lads from the other farms, as the labourers on the farms were getting 10½ d. an hour overtime pay. So I asked for 1s. for the lads, but the boss said he would give us 11d. which I refused, but after about an hour's argument he promised to pay 1s. an hour for hay-time and harvest and 11d. for all other overtime. So the lads were pleased about getting overtime pay. There was no farm workers' union in those days.

In wintertime, before we went to work in the fields, we lads had to help to feed 70 to 100 bullocks that were kept in the fold yards (mostly under cover) at each farm. When they were big enough they were sold to the butchers for beef. After seven years with the same boss he stopped me one day and asked if I had ever thought of getting married, as I had been courting the parlour maid who lived in and worked for the boss's wife, for three to four years. The boss said he was moving the foreman I lived with to another farm. So he would like me to take his place and be foreman at the farm I worked on. So after a long talk I said I would, if my young lady agreed to get married. She did and I came to live in the cottage where I had lived with the other foreman. That year (1938) I was hired for £52 and the boss gave me all of it and said he would give me £2 4s. 6d. a week for my wages. After I got married we were allowed free milk and potatoes and also free rent since it was a tied cottage that went with the job. I stayed and worked for the same boss until I retired.

CHAPTER FOURTEEN

PUTTING ON THE THATCH

Now that the harvest of memories has been gathered in and the stack built all that remains to be done is the thatching and the job will be completed. As the editor of these memoirs, gathered like sheaves from the field, I have tried to keep my comments to a minimum so as to allow the contributors full freedom to tell their stories in their own way. I trust that the stack I have built is a tidy one and now I seek to present a few ideas that have occurred to me in the course of my work. The material collected here opens a doorway into a lost world and preserves for future generations unique and intimate views of life in a bygone age.

One of the conclusions that may be drawn from this study relates to the selectivity of human memory. Given that the life-style described here may seem harsh and uncomfortable, it may be a surprise to find that almost all the informants, including those not reported in this book, indicated that they had happy lives in their youth. It is common to find people of this generation referring to 'the good old days' or saying 'life was hard but we enjoyed ourselves'. Most correspondents have an idyllic view of life in the village community of the past, and one old lady remarked that 'people were more caring in those days'. On the other hand some described the harsh treatment they received as children from schoolmasters and other adults, or the rough treatment farm workers received from their employers. The ill-treatment of women is also described by some writers. However, the general picture is of happy and contented people living quiet and peaceful lives in a situation which they often contrast with the noisy and conflict-filled lives of the present day.

To some extent our informants' perception of life may be accounted for by the process that the sociologist Runciman described as 'relative deprivation'. People tend to compare themselves with their neighbours who are in general in a similar social and economic position to themselves. In a situation in which an entire community suffers poverty the individual member of that community will not be likely to feel deprived.

Attitudes are influenced by the general ethos of the society in which people live. The inhabitants of an English village in the period before the Second World War were clearly aware of the existence of wealth even within their own communities, in the presence of 'the squire' and the 'big farmers' but they tended to see the class system as a part of the natural order. They did not aspire to emulate their 'betters' or indeed see any possibility of doing so. The most they aspired to was the possession of a smallholding. Most of them had no great expectations of achieving any significant improvement in their own standard of living and indeed in that period it was a struggle to maintain the standard of life they already had, low as it was. Those in work were constantly faced with the threat of unemployment and were always conscious of the fact that they were lucky to have a job. There was always a tendency to look down on the unemployed and on those who for one reason or another were unable to maintain a 'respectable place' in society. As a child I was frequently warned against talking to 'tramps' who were often seen on the roads making their way from one workhouse to another, and as one of our informants has described, gypsies were feared and hated.

I was surprised to find that few correspondents mentioned the Agricultural Workers' Union in spite of the fact that I wrote to the union's journal *The Land Worker* appealing for information from its readers.

Perhaps my own experience was in some ways unusual for both my maternal grandfather and my father were active trade unionists and supporters of the Labour movement. We took the Labour newspaper *The Daily Herald* and one of the few magazines I remember reading regularly was the *The Land Worker* generally recognized as one of the best union magazines ever published.

My grandfather Walter Pitcher had joined Joseph Arch's National Agricultural Labourers' Union when he was sixteen in 1879. The 'National' declined during the Great Depression and while a number of small local unions were formed there was little effective action until 1906 when George Edwards founded the Eastern Counties Agricultural Labourers' and Small Holders' Union which was to grow into The National Union of Agricultural Workers. Grandfather was one of the first to join that union, both he and my father were active members throughout their lives.

They were also both interested in politics. Before the formation of the Labour Party the Liberal Party provided the main outlet for the discontent of farm workers and was strongly supported in Norfolk where the farmers and landowners were naturally Conservative. My grandfather was threatened with eviction from his cottage for displaying a Liberal Party election poster but stuck to his principles. With the formation of the Labour Party most workers transferred their loyalty to that party, and in 1920 George Edwards was elected as the Labour Member of Parliament for the South West Norfolk constituency, which covered the district in which my family lived. George Edwards was highly venerated by farm workers and I remember as a small child being taken each year to the annual rally of the union held on Hempton Heath, Fakenham, and hearing him address an enthusiastic crowd as I sat on my father's shoulders.

Another important influence that has been scarcely mentioned by my correspondents is that of the Nonconformist chapels. There was a close connection between unionism and Primitive Methodism particularly in Norfolk. For instance George Edwards had learned many of his skills as a public speaker from his experience as a Methodist local preacher and this was the case with many of the other leaders of the Labour movement in rural areas. Other Nonconformist denominations such as Congregationalists, Baptists and Wesleyans were also strongly supported by workers in the rural areas, whereas these denominations were mainly supported by the middle class in urban areas.

Rural society was divided into several social classes and it is easy to distinguish between five social classes that could be found everywhere in the countryside:

1. The gentry; aristocrats, squires and landowners
2. Big farmers
3. Professionals; doctors, clergymen, lawyers, etc.
4. Small farmers, shopkeepers, craftsmen, etc.
5. Farm workers

However, this omits a factor that to some extent cuts across the others, a social rather than an economic factor, and one which was demonstrated most directly in religious and political allegiance. In most villages, certainly in Norfolk, but also in many other parts of the country the community was divided into Anglican/Conservatives on one hand and Nonconformists/Liberals on the other. The first three of the classes described above tending to be Anglican/Conservative. The fourth class tended to be Nonconformist/Liberal, but the workers were divided and two distinct classes of workers can be distinguished. My parents divided their class in two groups which they described as the 'respectable' and the 'scruffs'. As may be imagined they defined themselves as respectable. Respectable people went to chapel and were politically conscious, that is to say they were active trade unionists, and supporters of the Liberal or later the Labour Party. The scruffs supported very little apart from the public house, though some of them attended the church to ingratiate themselves with their employers and we suspected that they also voted for the Conservatives. I was forbidden to play with some local children because my parents defined them as scruffs.

While readers will have noticed some difference in the style of life in the various parts of the country that are reflected in these reminiscences, they will also have found that the similarities are much greater than the differences. For example most contributors give some account of the work of the horseman; the role and status of that job was remarkably constant in all parts of the country, though the title attached differs from 'team man' in some districts to wagoner or carter in others.

The conditions of work, the close contact with animals and the land led to a love of the soil, of nature and wildlife as well as the animals they worked with. This is clearly demonstrated in many of these memoirs. The attitude of the farm worker to his job was very different from that of the factory worker for they got greater satisfaction from their work. The farm worker of that period was not tied down to one repetitive process but had to be a master of many trades, a good worker could, as one correspondent remarked, 'turn his hand to anything on the farm'. Of course there were specialized farms and specialized jobs on general farms, such as horseman, cowman and shepherd and on big farms these men would be limited to their specific job. But within these specilizations there were a great number of processes involved. The horseman was not only in charge of the horses but was responsible for ploughing, sowing and reaping and any other task that involved the use of a horse. He also had to be able to care for the horses when they were sick or injured and act as a mid-wife when a foal was being born. He might also on some farms be expected to help with other jobs such as hedge laying.

As we have seen, farm workers took a great pride in their work and their status in the community depended to a considerable extent on the quality of their workmanship. The man who could plough the straightest furrow was greatly admired and indeed envied by the other local ploughmen, as was the stacker or rick-builder who could build the best stack, the thatcher who did the finest thatching, or the hedger who could lay the neatest hedge. These men working to the best of their ability with their own hands got great satisfaction out of their work.

Each of these stories gives a picture of country life as seen by a particular individual but taken together they enable us to see the broader picture of life as it was lived in England during the first half of the twentieth century.

FURTHER READING

I have made no attempt to compile a complete list of published memoirs of country life in the first half of the twentieth century or of other relevant books but have simply listed those books which I have read and which I believe may be of interest to readers.

Archer, Fred,   Author of a series of books all originally published by Hodder & Stoughton and including the following titles:
Under the Parish Lantern, 1969
The Secrets of Bredon Hill, 1971
A Lad of Evesham Vale, 1972
Muddy Boots and Sunday Suits, 1973
The Distant Scene, 1967
Golden Sheaves and Black Horses, 1974
When Village Bells were Silent, 1975

Arnold, J.,   *The Shell Book of Country Crafts*, Baker, London, 1968

Badcock, J.C.,   *The Four-Acre*, Dent, London, 1967

Bell, Adrian,   *Corduroy*, Penguin Books,
                       Harmondsworth, 1940
                       Sunrise to Sunset , John Lane,
                       London, 1944
                       The Budding Morrow, John Lane,
                       London, 1946

Bonnett, Harold,   *Farming With Steam*, Shire
                       Publications, 1974

Brigden, Roy,   *Ploughs and Ploughing*, Shire
                       Publications, 1984

Brooke, Justin   *Suffolk Prospect*, Faber, London,
and Edith,   1963

Burrows, Ray,   *Beckery Burrows*, Research
                       Publishing, London, 1978
                       Bide Awhile wi' I (Somerset Dialect
                       Poems), published by author, 1980

Chapman, D.H.,   *Farmer Jim*, Harrap, London, 1944

Chapman, Hubert,   *A Village Upbringing*, printed by
                       Advance Offset, Hitchen, 1979

Copper, Bob,   *A Song for Every Season*,
                       Heinemann, 1971

Cowley, Violet,   *Over My Shoulder*, Stockwell,
                       Ilfracombe, 1985

Edwards, George,   *From Crow-scaring to Westminster*, Labour Publishing Co., London, 1922

Evans, George Ewart,   *Where Beards Wag All*, Faber, London, 1970

Evans, Simon,   *The Poet Postman*, Kenneth Tomkinson, Kidderminster, 1981

Gardner, C.H.,   *Your Village and Mine*, Faber, London, 1944

Geere, Marjorie,   *Reminiscences of a Land Girl in Witham*, A. Poulter, Witham, Essex, 1987

Groves, R.,   *Sharpen the Sickle*, Merlin Press, London, 1981

Harman, R., (ed.)   *Countryside Mood*, Blandford Press, London, 1943

Harris, Mollie,   *Cotswold Privies*, Chatto and Windus, London, 1984
Farm Acre End, Chatto and Windus, London, 1986

Henderson, G.,   *The Farming Ladder*, Faber, London, 1944

FURTHER READING

Hill, Susan,   *The Magic Apple Tree*, Penguin Books, 1983

Hillyer, Richard, *Country Boy*, Hodder & Stoughton, London, 1967

Hodgekinson, W.P., *The Eloquent Silence*, English Universities Press, 1946

Home, Michael, *Autumn Fields*, Methuen, London, 1944

How, R.W.,   *Good Country Days*, Hollis and Carter, London, 1946

Jennings, P.,   *The Living Village*, Hodder & Stoughton, London, 1968

Kent, Joan,   *Binder Twine and Rabbit Stew*, Bailey Brothers & Swinfen, Folkestone, 1976

Ketteridge, Christopher and Spike Mays, *Five Miles from Bunkum*, Eyre Methuen, London, 1972

Lockley, R.H.,   *Inland Farm*, Witherby, London, 1943

Lovesey, Edward, *A Postman's Tales*, the author, Gaydon, Warwick, 1987

Megginson, Irene, *Mud On My Doorstep*, Hutton Press, Beverley, 1987

Middleton, C.H., *Village Memories*, Cassell, London, 1941

Moore, John, *A Portrait of Elmbury*, Collins, London, 1945

Nial, Ian, *The Village Policeman*, Heinemann, London, 1971

Page, Warrenton, *Holbrook, The Story of a Village 1900–83*, The Pentland Press, Edinburgh, 1983

Ready, Oliver, *A Countryman on The Broads*, MacGibbon and Kee, London, 1967

Refford, Harry, *Pie For Breakfast*, Hutton Press, Beverley, 1984

Rose, Walter and John Hockham, *Good Neighbours*, Cambridge University Press, 1942

Scott, Wilfred, *To a Farmer Born*, Bristol Broadsides, 1987

Scott-Watson, J.A., *The Farming Year*, Longman Green, London

Smith, D.J.,   *Horse Drawn Farm Machines*, Shire
                            Publications, 1984

Stewart, Sheila,   *Lifting the Latch*, Oxford
                            University Press, 1986

Strange, Alf,   *Me Dad's a Village Blacksmith*, Gee
                            and Son, Denbigh, 1983
                            Following Me Dad, Gee and Son,
                            Denbigh, 1986

Street, A.G.,   *Strawberry Roan*, Faber, London,
                            1932
                            Round The Year On The Farm,
                            Oxford University Press, London,
                            1942

Swinford, George,   *The Jubilee Boy*, The Filkins Press,
                            Lechlade, 1988

Taylor, J.W.,   *Reminiscences of a Fenman*, published
                            by the author, Tilney All Saints,
                            King's Lynn

Thompson, Flora,   *Lark Rise to Candleford*, Oxford
                            University Press, 1939

Thompson, John,   *Horse-Drawn Farm Vehicles*,
                            J. Thompson, Fleet, Hampshire,
                            1980

Tylden, G.,   *Harness and Saddlery*, Shire Publications, 1971

Uttley, Alison,   *The Country Child*, Faber, London, 1931
Country Things, Faber, London, 1946

Vince, J.,   *Carts and Wagons*, Shire Publications, 1987

Webb, Henry,   *Advanced Agriculture*, Longman, Green, London, 1894

Webber, Ronald,   *The Village Blacksmith*, David and Charles, 1971

White, E.G.,   *And Flour Came in Ten Stone Sacks*, the author, Coalfield, Bury St Edmunds, 1986

Whitlow, Ralph,   *A Family and a Village*, J. Baker, 1969

Whyte, Betsy,   *The Yellow on the Broom*, Chambers, Edinburgh, 1979

Wightman, R.,   *Wallace's Ground*, Pelham Books, 1971

Williams, James,   *Give Me Yesterday*, Country Book Club, 1973

FURTHER READING

Williamson,
Henry,

The Story Of A Norfolk Farm,
Faber, London, 1941